# The Summer of Paintless

*Toenails*

LOSING A SON—GAINING A GRANDSON
ONE AWESOME GRANDMA MAKING A DIFFERENCE

SAMUEL LEE &
DEBRA SUSAN BOWMAN

# THE SUMMER OF PAINTLESS *Toenails*
LOSING A SON—GAINING A GRANDSON ONE AWESOME GRANDMA
MAKING A DIFFERENCE

Printed in the USA

ISBN (print): 978-0-9983494-2-8

ISBN (kindle): 978-0-9983494-3-5

Library of Congress Control Number: 2017937012

Published by The Bowman Initiative | Sharpsville, Indiana                    |

Scripture taken from King James version is taken specifically from the Thompson Chain Reference Bible, © Copyright 1964 by B.B. Kirkbride Bible Company, Inc. Used by permission.

Scripture take from the NIV Topical Study Bible, © Copyright 1989 by the Zondervan Corporation. Used by permission.

Scripture taken from the Amplified Bible, © Copyright 1987, by The Lockman Foundation. www.lockman,org. Used by permission.

Any words added to a scripture by the authors are noted as such and appear in brackets.

To Contact the Authors:

www.bowmanitiative.com

www.awesomegrandmothers.org

# DEDICATION

To all the godly, praying grandmothers who have given so much to save a generation—this book is for you.

To Sara Hale and Maggie Bowman—two super mothers who did it all and gave us the lives we have.

# PRAISE FOR THE SUMMER OF PAINTLESS TOENAILS

*The Summer of Paintless Toenails* may sound like a cute little fairytale, until you start reading it. Grandparents, Sam and Debbie Bowman, have turned their loss and heartache into hope for themselves and hundreds of other grandparents who are raising their grandchildren. Read this book and check out awesomegrandmothers.org and you will no longer walk alone.

~LOGAN SPARLING
*Pastor, founder Christian Fellowship International*

As Sam and Debbie's pastor, friend and former co-radio host, I can say by experience, they are engaging and have a tremendous heart for ministry to the Lord and to people.

~PASTOR RON MEYER
*Pastor, Harmony Christian Church*

What can I say ? I'm honored to be a part of the heart healing that Sam and Debbie are embarking upon. The book speaks to my heart as I recall the hours Deb and I spent sharing the joys and heartaches of being mothers of strong willed sons. Laughing and crying together, hugging and hoping for their futures. And the agony all of us who had worked side by side . . day in and out while raising our children . . . shared when we got the call to prayer at Zachary's death. For many years we had shared joys and pain of motherhood . . . this too we would share, if only to lighten Deb's burden. So it is with joy I share this healing too. Thank you Deb and you Sam, you're both the bomb-diggity.

~VICKI MOORE
*Nurse, Colleague, Friend, Avid Supporter*

This book is loving ministry in a touching, emotional and heartfelt story. The authors share deepening insights from personal journeys God placed in their hearts.

~LEEANN WALLSMITH
*RN, RDCS*
*Forever Friend (with or without polished toenails)*

With honest vulnerability, Sam and Debbie intimately open their hearts, sharing their journey of steadfast faith and trust in God through tragedy, heartache, loss and disease. Their lives are a testament of His grace and mercy, as they minister hope to grandparents, parents and children with God's healing love. Interwoven between the pages of their journey, you will weep and laugh, discover hope and joy, receive wisdom and be strengthened in your faith to "rest" in the promises of God's Word. Sam and Debbie have a passionate love for their Savior, who has turned their mourning into dancing! Their story will encourage your hearts to trust in Jesus through your journey--joy comes in the morning!

~SYLVIA GRANT
*Long-time Friend, Prayer Partner*

Sam and Debbie Bowman have been personal friends of ours for many years. As ministers, the Summer of Paintless Toenails: Losing a son, gaining a son, helps you understand the people who have lost loved ones and how to minister to them. We admire them for their strong faith in the Lord and the perseverance to live victorious when bad things happen in life.

~JEANNE COOK
*Pastor, Evangelist, Missionary to Panama*

*The Summer of Paintless Toenails* is an incredibly honest and heartfelt journey. Samuel and Debra boldly open up their lives and their hearts with one mission in mind - to provide hope and support for heroic grandparents that have taken on the challenge of raising their grandchildren. This book will surely be a blessing to grandparents everywhere!

~LAUREN BERCARICH
*Communications Director, Liquid Church*

In all my life, there has never been a more stable female influence as Debbie. Even though she may technically be my step-mother, I am so proud to call her Mom. She continually shows compassion, empathy and love to all of those around her. She always points people to Christ. And, she cares beyond the imaginable. There is no one better to write a book about loss and grief, losing and gaining, and standing firm in Christ when it is impossible for us to stand on our own. She has lived it. She has experienced it. She has survived it. I'm so glad she is sharing that with the world.

~KIMBERLY BOWMAN LOWE
*CEO Kagan Korea*
*Delight of a Daughter, Friend, Wonderful Mother to our Loved Grace and Ethan*

# Table of Contents

---

*Introduction*                           1

Chapter One
*A Hard Knock Knock*                      5

Chapter Two
*Look Up Daughter*                        15

Chapter Three
*On That Distant Shore*                   25

Chapter Four
*A Walton's Family Rerun*                 35

Chapter Five
*Into the Blender*                        45

Chapter Six
*In Sickness and in Health*              53

Chapter Seven
*The Life We Choose*                      65

Chapter Eight
*The Life we Lose*                        75

Chapter Nine
*The Religion Factor*      87

Chapter Ten
*A Summer Place*      97

Chapter Eleven
*Falling off the Bicycle*      105

Chapter Twelve
*Getting Back on the Bicycle*      113

Chapter Thirteen
*Connections*      123

Chapter Fourteen
*Recovery Room*      133

Appendix
*Let's Connect*      145

# Introduction

---

## A WORD FROM DEBBIE

*This* is the journal of our journey and a window into the depths of our hearts. What we will reveal to you here we will do for the healing of our own hearts and for the encouragement of your heart. It's a chronicle of all Sam and I have been through; the lengthy death of a spouse, the sudden death of a small child and the loss of a grown adult child. It is a story of losing one family and the merging of two new families. It is the story of drug addiction and I-need-to-fix-everything addiction. It is about a mom, meaning well, taking on the burdens only God should carry. It's also about victory over drugs, death, diapers, depression and the challenges that often come with them. It's about finding a journey to faith, hope and joy amid the ashes of death and despondency. Our story is an all too common story in this day and age, one you might have gone through or may be in the midst of at this very moment.

At sixty years of age I was forced to retire from a rewarding career in nursing, from which I had gained so much satisfaction and much of my identity. I found myself planning a funeral and buying diapers. Life had suddenly pulled me from the bliss of being a grandmother back into the challenging reality of being a mother.

In the following days, Sam and I had to rethink our whole lives. We had to give up many of our hopes and dreams. As spring turned into summer and the flip-flops came out I noticed my unpainted toenails and thought, I need to get them painted and a pedicure. Then I thought, no, I feel so depressed. I didn't feel like doing anything for myself. At that moment I thought I will always remember this as the summer of the paintless toenails and if I ever write a book that's what I'll call it. Well, ta-da! Here it is.

## A WORD FROM SAM

*First* off I just want to say I have to wonder if this is a title for a book that us guys would want to read. But, hey, I love to get along with my wife and this is the title she came up with, so the title of this book is *The Summer of Paintless Toenails.*

I just want you dad's and grandpa's to know this book is for you too. I'll be saying a few things from my perspective in this journal. After all, this family affair is not only about what the woman goes through, but what the man goes through too, and there is also the dynamic of what you experience as a team when you face things like death and diapers at the ripe old age of sixty.

So here we go writing a book together and wondering if it's going to be like wallpapering, which is known to be a challenge to any relationship. In the wallpaper business it's called the marriage wrecker! But hey, we have wallpapered together and we're still married, and writing together can't be worse than losing a child, and we've done that together too.

It can be very challenging to be the spiritual leader of a put together family. Trying to get two sets of kids to like each other when they've been used to having mom or dad all to themselves can be like mixing oil and water. Not easy!

Debbie and I have been counselors for each other dealing with so many issues: combining family, caring for the next generation, keeping healthy borders, dealing with guilt and shame, defeating depression and other daily challenges. We often bump fists when we get a little victory and ask each other, quoting the Tom Cruise movie Oblivion, "Are we an effective team?" The answer is a resounding yes, but it's been a process. I'll be sharing a lot about how grandpa's can keep the kids, or grandkids, from burning down the house all while forging a powerful team with your wife.

## THE VOICE OF PAINTLESS TOENAILS

Since both Sam and Debbie have a voice in this writing it could be confusing as to who is speaking, so we are going to preface sections with our name to help with clarity. In some cases either way works, so take it whichever way makes sense for you.

## FOR GRANDMOTHER AND MOTHERS

This book is pointed toward helping and encouraging awesome grandmothers, but, of course, the lessons and principles can work just as well for mothers. So, whichever you are take the subject as meant for you, no matter which title we might use.

## CHILDREN AND GRANDCHILDREN

Also, whether we use the term children or grandchildren, know that whichever term is used that it covers all the generations after you.

## SAM AND DEBBIE

We have the promise that all things work together for good, so we know it's not over till it's all good and everything just keeps getting better and better for us and it will for you, too.

So, next summer when the flip-flops come out, so will the painted toenails! Maybe while Debbie gets her toenails done Sam will go deep sea fishing.

# Chapter One

# A Hard Knock Knock

## DEBBIE

*It* was what every parent fears and my worst night ever, April 24, 2014. The pounding at the door came at 10:00 p.m. I opened my eyes and saw a light pattern on the wall beside my head. Someone was parked in our driveway with their brights on. I swung my drowsy feet from under the cozy blankets, pulled on a robe and went for a peep through the front window blinds. Two policemen were standing at our front door. My heart sank. Now what? I instinctively knew it had to be Zachary, our thirty-five-year-old son. We had been through so much over the years with Zachary and lately he had seemed more on edge than usual, like a caged animal, pacing and pawing.

## CHAIN OF EVENTS

I had been at this juncture with Zachary so many times before; trips to the emergency room, juvenile detention, youth homes, wondering where he was at midnight and who was turning into our driveway at three in the morning, finally graduating to bailouts at the county jail. Somehow, deep in my heart, I knew the long, long ordeal was finally over.

Just two weeks before Zachary had approached me and asked, "Mom, if anything ever happens to us will you and Sam take care of Anthony?" I didn't think too much of it at the time, just a young father concerned about his son I supposed. He and Anthony had been close. I have no doubt he loved him dearly. I said, "I'm sure we would" never thinking it would ever really happen and most certainly, not so soon. I don't know if he saw something coming, but it became a prophetic question, fulfilled on this night of terrible, bad news.

The chain of events began three days earlier. I was excited to have a few days off from the long, demanding hours of being an RN in intensive care. Then I came down with the stomach flu. How exciting was that! I remember thinking at least I didn't have to run after a toddler while I was puking. I never dreamed my world was about to turn upside down and drop a toddler into my lap.

In a day or so I was feeling a little better, and since Sam was out of town on business, I decided to go down to Zachary's trailer and see our grandkids, Bella (5) and Anthony (then 18 months). When I arrived his fiancée was suffering the stomach flu too, so I really felt for her. Zachary was there and at near hysterics saying he had been robbed at gunpoint downtown where he went for counseling. I felt bad for them, so I offered to take both kids for the night. I'd never had them both overnight. Anthony had just stopped taking seizure medication and his wide mood swings made him a challenge. But I knew how bad she must be feeling. They gladly bundled them up and I set off for my house with both kids. As it turns out, in God's providence, it

---
**GOD'S HAND IS OFTEN HIDDEN IN THE SIMPLE DECISIONS**
---

saved their lives. God's hand is often hidden in the simple decisions we make. Had they been out with their parents that night surely one or both of them would have been killed along with their father.

I cracked open the front door and said, "Yes?"

They asked, "Are you Debra Bowman, Zachary Butts' mother?"

I said, "Yes" and opened the door to let them come in.

They asked if there was a place we could sit down. I knew what they were going to say.

The officers were so compassionate. "There has been a car crash," one said and I began to recede somewhere into the distance, into a heavy fog that was already settling across my mind. One of them said Zachary was driving and attempted to pass a car and hit another car head on. He was lifelined to Methodist Hospital in Indianapolis where he later died. His fiancée was with him and had also been lifelined and remained in critical condition.

## LIKE A GOOD NEIGHBOR— OUR GOD IS THERE!

People don't know their neighbors anymore like they used to. Where does anyone turn at a moment like this when they don't have neighbors to call on, or family to lean on? From where does the comfort come for a broken heart and a fractured life?

The policeman asked me if there was anyone I could call. I moved to the couch and looked at my hand and saw a phone there I didn't even remember holding. I told them my good friends, Debbie and Jerry, lived just across the street so they went to get them for me. I remember thinking what a nightmare for them having the police come to the door in the middle of the night, but I needed them and, like so many times before, I knew they would be there for me.

Soon our long-time friend Pastor Logan arrived, who had preached my first husband's funeral and then led Sam and I as we said our wedding vows. This time great comfort came through the same door that just a little while before had opened to so much sorrow. So many tears had been wrenched from my heart so many times before with this child, who I had prayed over and grieved over time and time again. I had always believed God would answer my prayer to completely heal my son. I just never thought He would have to ultimately do it by taking him from this life, from me.

## PUT YOUR SEAT BACKS IN THE UPRIGHT POSITION AND PREPARE FOR DEPARTURE

No parent should have to bury their children. It's supposed to be the other way around. Just the same, we must all let go of our children and place them into God's hands for we never know what the next day will hold. While we are preparing them for our eventual departure, it is also wise to prepare ourselves to let go of our children. This is not about living in fear. It's about living in faith, but with wisdom to be prepared for any eventuality. We must continue to pray, believe for the best, think the best and hope for the best, no matter what happens, but it doesn't always go the way we envision. We must be spiritually prepared to let go of our children, but not just let go of them. We must release them to a place, and the only truly safe place is into the hands of almighty God, who is big enough and wise enough to do what is best for them, to open up heaven if need be, even if that leaves us feeling like hell back here on earth.

## HOW DOES AN OPTIMIST PREPARE FOR THE WORST?

How does an optimist prepare for the worst? They take the time to instill habits, develop skills and invest in knowledge that will give them the power to make the best of the worst. The same skills that enable them to succeed are the same skills that can make something good out of any opportunity that comes along, good, bad or indifferent. There are two things successful people know how to do, in both business and in personal life; they never, ever give up, no matter what, and they make the best of whatever happens, no matter what. These people are always in training for what may come at any time.[1]

I walked back to the bedroom and looked down at the two innocent, sweet children sleeping soundly, unaware they would never see their father again, wondering how we would tell them and how they would take it. Would they, could they, understand? Would their lives be shattered? Would they ever recover? What would their wounding look like and how would they be healed?

So began what I would come to call the summer of paintless toenails. In the weeks that followed I just didn't feel like getting dressed up or putting on any makeup. My appetite was gone. I lost ten pounds. Yet, in the midst of the sorrow there came a peace that surpasses all understanding. It is in times like this

## GOOD GRIEF

I am convinced of the importance of keeping at the task of nurturing one's faith because I have seen how such people demonstrate greatness under trial. Conversely, I have seen what happens to people who have not taken seriously the necessity of working at their faith when the going was good. These people seem unprepared to handle even the small losses which face all of us from time to time.

People of faith do not just suddenly get that way. Like the athlete who must stay in training, these people are always in training for whatever may come at any time. When loss comes they are ready for it. It is just one of many griefs they have learned to wrestle with creatively.

—GRANGER E WESTBERG
*Good Grief*

that you can take a harvest from what you have sown. I drew upon my faith in God and it sustained me.

> *". . . you whom I have upheld since you were conceived,*
> *and have carried since your birth. Even to your old age*
> *and gray hairs I am he, I am he who will sustain you."*
> ISAIAH 46:3-4 (NIV)

## WHAT'S IN A MARRIAGE?

Many marriages do not survive a catastrophic event like this. The event magnifies whatever is already resident in the relationship. It's like tossing a stick of dynamite into your heart and whatever is in there is blown out, into real life, into the public eye. It can't stay in. Sam went through this in his first marriage and they were not able to survive. When you are not close, the disaster will blow you apart. When you are close the disaster will drive you together. Fortunately, Sam and I have always been close and so we went hyper close. God gave us great peace, comfort and even a measure of joy during the funeral. Logan and Sam preached a great message and many were touched.

## DRAWING ON YOUR FAITH ACCOUNT

A lot of people saw our peace and joy in the midst of the sorrow and asked us how we did it. The answer was simple and obvious to us. We trusted God. Both of us have believed that Jesus was who He said He was, the son of God, and we have given our hearts to Him. Now He is in us and He works in us to help, counsel, comfort and love. We have found Him to be oh so very real in every part of our lives and in every moment of our lives, the good and the bad. Sam said to someone, "We have a faith bank account and we have been making deposits for a long time. Now we have a place to go to make a withdrawal when we need it." That's exactly what we did. The years of praying, believing, growing in the knowledge of the Word and God brings great strength in moments like these and this is the faith that will carry us on to whatever conclusion life may hold, and through all the ups and downs between now and then.

There is no hope, if there is no God, for if there is no God who can rescue us, hold us, comfort us, heal us and save us from being forever dead after death? Without Him there is nothing worth hoping in. Everything will eventually fail us. Sam and I can confidently say, there is help, hope and healing in the midst of the heartache. It's supernatural. It just arrives. It flows and it comes with abundance. We know. We've been there and the Holy Spirit never fails to deliver when you trust in Jesus.

In the words of the old hymn:

> *My hope is built on nothing less*
> *Than Jesus' blood and righteousness;*
> *I dare not trust the sweetest frame,*
> *But wholly lean on Jesus' name.*
> *On Christ, the solid Rock, I stand;*
> *All other ground is sinking sand.*
>
> *When darkness seems to hide His face,*
> *I rest on His unchanging grace;*
> *In every high and stormy gale,*
> *My anchor holds within the veil.*
> *On Christ, the solid Rock, I stand;*
> *All other ground is sinking sand.*
> *All other ground is sinking sand.*[2]

In times of great distress you look one of two ways for answers, you look without to what this world has to offer, or you look within, to what your soul has to offer. Sam and I looked within, for residing there was a comfort not of ourselves. His name was Jesus. He can come to live in your heart and release to you what you need in any season.

In times like this there are two friends that stick closer than a brother; the scripture and the writer of the scripture, the Holy Spirit. They are a fountain of comfort and rest that flows.

## The Rest of the Story

During this season of despondency the Holy Spirit gave me rest every day. Like cool, refreshing water, He flowed over me and soaked into the sorrow that filled my soul. Eventually the trickle became a flow as I rested upon the river and let it carry me through.

So, we make a to-do list and keep going, one foot in front of the other, day by day. Sometimes we have to live hour by hour, simply living out our moments ever watching for our Lord to reveal Himself in the midst of our movements.

*"My presence shall go with thee, and I will give thee rest."*
EXODUS 33:14 (KJV)

## ENDNOTES

1. Westberg, Granger E. Fortress Press, Philadelphia, © Copyright 1962, ISBN 0-8006-1114-4, page 62.
2. *The Lutheran Hymnal*, Hymn number 370, from I Timothy 1:1, Composer John Stainer, 1873.

## Debbie's To Do List ———————→

☑   Buy Diapers

☑   Pick up Some Sippy Cups

☑   Plan Funeral

☑   Lay on the Bed and Cry

☑   Play in the Yard with the Kids

☑   Ask God Why?

☑   Do Some Laundry

THERE IS HELP, HOPE AND
HEALING IN THE MIDST
OF THE HEARTACHE

## Chapter Two

# *Look Up Daughter*

··· ❧ ❧ ···

## DEBBIE

*My* first summer of paintless toenails was put in motion in the spring of 1972 when I married my high school sweetheart.

Tom was a handsome, outgoing young man. I met him at a basketball game between our rival high schools. He asked for my number and I gave him the wrong one, on purpose. I was afraid he might actually call and I didn't want my parents privy to our relationship. My parents were very principled people and Tom was a smooth operator. I craved the attention. The affection grew and two years later I found a new life growing inside me.

In the summer I walked across the stage to get my high school diploma, seven months pregnant. It was not an easy thing to do back in those days. It was a big social no-no to get pregnant out of wedlock and even more taboo to present it in public at school. I loved the baby that was growing in me so much that I didn't care what other people thought. I was one of the very first to be allowed to go through the public graduation ceremony at my high school with an obvious baby on board. Some of the sting was abated since Tom and I had married a couple of months before graduation, but it was a very hard time for my parents and I have always felt the backlash of letting them down.

# BUILDING A FAMILY

Our little girl Stacy arrived and with a lot of help from our two families we were able to hold it together. I naively believed the future would be all good, but the first five years were very rocky. I was going to school, working and caring for Stacy while Tom got into the drug and party scene with his friends. I felt like I was taking care of one infant in the diaper scene and another one in the drug scene.

In those first tumultuous years God began to sneak up on both Tom and I, from different angles and in different ways. My parents had raised me in a Methodist church. I believed in God and knew the Bible as his Word, but as time went along I began to sense a growing hunger in me for a more intimate relationship with Him. I had met friends in college who were asking questions about life and seeking answers. They planted spiritual seeds in me that began to grow.

On the other hand, Tom was raised in a very strict, conservative church. His activities were simply rebellion toward his parents. He played the keyboards for a band and the guys began to ask questions about God. His hunger for something more grew and Tom found himself in conflict over who he would serve; God or the party life. But the hunger grew and while he was seeking God he would smoke pot and watch the 700 Club on cable TV.

# GIVING OUR HEARTS TO JESUS

A friend at work, invited me to attend Morning Star church, where I went down front to the altar and gave my heart to Jesus. I cried until my mascara ran down my face. I remember telling someone close by the tears were bad for the mascara, but good for the soul. In the following days my love for the Bible, the Word of God, grew. I found new friends at the church and experienced a peace I had never known.

I began to invite Tom to go with me and eventually talked him into going to a Bible study. He was willing because it was being led by a man who also played in a band. I remember the first time we went we drove around the block a few times because Tom was afraid to go in. Finally, he gave in and soon after followed me to the altar at Morning Star, where he gave his life to the Lord.

When Tom gave his heart to Jesus it was a complete turn around. He gave up his drugs and all his old friends. Actually he ran a few of them off. He'd tell them Jesus is the greatest high you'll ever know and that's the last we'd see of them. Our relationship made an abrupt turn for the better and in the next five years our marriage vastly improved. After ten years, when people would ask Tom how long we had been married, he would say, "Five happy years."

Our second child, Zachary, arrived on Valentine's day 1979, about seven years into our marriage. Those were good years after our commitment to the Lord. As our tenth anniversary passed I felt positive about the future and my hopes were high that things would turn out well between Tom and I, and for our family.

# A NEW KIND OF TROUBLE

Then the unthinkable happened. I never dreamed I'd be a widow at thirty-two.

The first sign of trouble was tingling in the tips of Tom's fingers and he began to have trouble playing the keyboards for the new Christian band he'd become part of. As it progressed he said it sometimes felt as if the center of his body was wrapped in cellophane. Then came trouble with his vision. He was eventually diagnosed with Multiple Sclerosis. It began a long, progressive downhill slide. We later found it to be chronic progressive M.S. with no remissions.

One of the doctors used to always say good-by to him by saying be cool. Tom would look back and say if you look up cool in the dictionary you'll see a picture of me. He could barely talk by that time, but he would laugh hysterically at his own jokes. No matter how bad it got he always kept his sense of humor. It was one of his best coping mechanisms.

I got him a golden retriever to help keep him company during the long days by himself while I worked and cared for the kids, but it wasn't a great idea. He could never get Daisy to dial 911 and instead of delivering his slippers all she did was chew them. Tom would say when he fell down the dog would just stand there and wag its tail, but she did do one thing well, she gave us a great case of the fleas.

During those long days he would watch the 700 Club. Once he was all excited because he made a ten-dollar one-time pledge and then he found an envelope that had a hundred dollars in it.

Our parents and Tom's brothers would come help exercise his legs. People from church visited and wrote cards. One creative fellow made a card that said in big letters on the front, to Tom Terrific and filled the inside with a super hero story of one Tom Terrific who was living life to the fullest and spitting death in the eye. He kept it on the end table and laughed when he saw it. One time one of the men at church even came and got Tom and carried him and his wheel chair out to his shop, where he covered him with blankets so he could watch him work.

# ROCK MY WORLD

When God speaks it is awesome. It will rock your world. God's language is flowing from His throne all of the time. It vibrates to the whole universe, to everything; every planet, every atom, and every living thing. It is part of His most essential nature to be communicating with His creation, with His loved ones. But the question is, am I listening? As surely as He is built to speak, you and I are built to hear, to see, to absorb His words. He is ever transferring to us His love, and the encouragement we need to succeed in life.

God speaks on many levels. He whispers in the peace of our inner soul. He talks to us in the midst of our problems and conflicts. He screams to us in the excruciating pain of our brokenness and failure. His precious whispers are often drowned out by the daily noise of TV, radio, internet and traffic. Virtually every place you go the air is filled with sound of some kind. Every business plays music over their loud speaker system. Somehow, in an effort to fill the void of our souls we fill our ears and eyes, even all our senses, stuffed to overflowing with sound, so we might not have to face and admit the emptiness of our hearts. But God is relentless in His search for those who will tune to Him.

Sometimes His voice can be so stark, so clear, so powerful, it trumps all of the clamor and clatter bombarding us and comes through as clear as someone standing beside us. It usually is a T-bone type experience. By that I mean it comes when you're not looking for it, it just T-bones you out of the blue. That's because it's nothing created in the logic of your own mind, it just comes from His mind directly to yours, trumping the overload of sensory perception that might be taking place at that moment.

Tom was playing the keyboards while the band was singing a song Rex Byers, the leader of the band, had written. He sang the words:

*I was with you in the beginning*
*I will be with you until the end*
*I am with you . . .*

We were worshiping. My hands were in the air. My eyes were closed. Rex sang "I am with you" and suddenly His words penetrated my soul so strongly it was as if someone leaned into my ear and spoke them from beside me, "Look up daughter." I turned to see who was there, but no one was close enough who could have spoken so clearly over the music. I instinctively knew it was the Lover Of My Soul, my Lord and my Savior.

It did not seem so powerful at the moment. I didn't cry or anything. I was just surprised that no one was there. However, over time the impact that God had spoken to me began to sink in. Many times God has used those words to take my eyes off my circumstances and put them where they should be, focused on His kind and loving face. They always touch my soul and make me feel so loved. They remind me that God is not just a set of rules, or a religion, but He is a person, a living being, who cares for me enough to whisper words designed just for me.

Time and time again, from that moment to this, I have pulled on them. A word from heaven spoken in a moment can penetrate our whole life from that moment forward. I would desperately need them in the days to come.

## THE SLIDE CONTINUES

Many people prayed and pleaded for Tom's recovery, but his M.S. continued to progress. Soon he was no longer able to play in the band.

Even though he was near totally incapacitated that final year he was never like one of my patients. We could no longer passionately kiss, but our passion for each other grew in those days and we were as close as we had ever been.

He had been sick for 5 years. It was difficult because just as soon as we got acclimated to one disability a new one would surface. Besides working as a nurse at the hospital and raising two kids, I became my husband's full-time-at-home caretaker. Once my sister-in-law asked me how we did it. I remember telling her from the depths of my heart that the answer was the *Footprints in the Sand.*[1]

> *One night I dreamed I was walking*
> *along the beach with the Lord.*
> *Many scenes from my life flashed across the sky.*
> *In each scene I noticed footprints in the sand.*
> *Sometimes there were two sets of footprints,*
> *other times there were one set of footprints.*
> *This bothered me because I noticed that during the low*
> *periods of my life, when I was suffering from anguish,*
> *sorrow or defeat, I could see only one set of footprints.*
> *So I said to the Lord, "You promised me Lord, that*
> *if I followed you, you would walk with me always.*
> *But I have noticed that during the most trying periods of*
> *my life there have only been one set of footprints in the sand.*
> *Why, when I needed you most, you have not been there for me?"*
> *The Lord replied, "The times when you have seen*
> *only one set of footprints, is when I carried you."*

When I was so tired I asked the Lord, "Where are you? There is only one set of footprints." He replied to me in the most personal way, "It was then my child that I carried you."

A month before Tom died I asked him about a ventilator if it came to that, he said, "Don't prolong my suffering." I was crying and he said "Don't cry." He could barely talk. He knew he had a heavenly home waiting for him with a new body. He underlined in his Bible many scriptures including this promise regarding Jesus and salvation:

> *"Who his own self bare our sins in his own body on*
> *the tree, that we, being dead to sins, should live unto*
> *righteousness: by whose stripes ye were healed."*
> 1 PETER 2:24 (KJV)

He knew that no matter which way it went, whether God healed Him or decided to take him on home, he would receive the ultimate healing, which he did!

I went to the chapel to pray as he lay dying and there was a stained glass that said a line from the Bible, the book of Deuteronomy, chapter thirty-three, verse twenty-seven:

## UNDERNEATH ARE THE EVERLASTING ARMS

This ministered to me because I felt like I was falling and wondering how life could go on. To know those arms were there to catch me and hold me was an amazing comfort.

After he died I felt pain in my heart, like I'd been stabbed. It was a real physical pain, in spite of my assurance that I'd see him again. I've heard people say the pain never goes away when someone dies. My experience is that while the memories and sense of loss are always there, the pain does lessen as I spend time snuggled, deeply resting, in the arms of my loving heavenly Father.

In his book *You Gotta Keep Dancing* Tim Hansel says, "Our level of joy (and therefore strength and healing) is directly proportional to our level of acceptance. Our attitude is the key."[2]

We were thirty-two years old when Tom changed bodies. I never dreamed I'd be a widow at that young age. At that time God showed me one thing very clearly; you have to keep on dancing.

## The Rest of the Story.

I read *Streams In the Desert*[3] after Tom died as a daily encouragement. So much of my time and energy had gone into caring for Tom so there was a big void in my life and daily routine. During those days God gave me the strength to keep going one step at a time. Caring for my kids gave me purpose. I found great rest in those days by drawing on God's promises of rest.

*"Come to me, all you who are weary and burdened, and I will give you rest."*
MATTHEW 11:28 (NIV)

## ENDNOTES

1. *Footprints In the Sand,* a poem by Mary Stevenson.
2. Tim Hansel, *You Gotta Keep Dancin'* (Elgin, Illinois: David C. Cook publishing company, 1985) page 105.
3. *Streams In The Desert* by Mrs. Charles E. Cowman.

# *Debbie's To Do List* ———✦

- ☑ Do the Dishes
- ☑ Keep on Dancing
- ☑ Get the Kids Off to School
- ☑ Lay on the Bed and Cry
- ☑ Cope with the Void
- ☑ Sort Through His Clothes
- ☑ Dust the Living Room

# Chapter Three

# On That Distant Shore

••• ❧⚜❧ •••

## SAM

*My* worst summer ever was the summer of 1981. It was way beyond a summer of paintless toenails. It began May 22nd.

At that time I was just getting started doing puppets as a hobby and ministry. Later on that hobby would grow to become my headache, as I like to say about the business, but that's another story. At this point in time I was traveling around doing children's ministry for churches. This particular week Lora (my first wife) and I traveled up north from our home in Peoria, Illinois, to present a special show at a school promoting a kids crusade at a local church we would be doing in the evenings. The church we were working for had made housing arrangements so Lora and the kids would have a place to stay during the day while I did the special appearances with the puppets.

I remember leaving Lora and the kids, Kimberly (then five), Cameron (then three), and Christopher (then two), at our assigned home early that morning to go set up for a late morning school show. A big crowd of kids had filed into the gym and soon after I began the program with my guitar a man entered the gym and walked right up to me in front of the crowd and said, "We need to leave right now and go the hospital. There has been an accident." I sat down my guitar, looked at the crowd and followed him off stage and out a side door. As he passed the person in charge he said, "Please take over. There has been an accident. Have the kids pray." I was shaken to the core.

## OFF TO THE HOSPITAL

As we raced off down the road I asked him what had happened. He said he did not know, but it had something to do with Christopher, Kit as we had nicknamed him. I asked him what the problem was or if it was serious. He said the hospital would not say, only to come right away. It's always a bad sign when they won't say anything about what's going on. I remember a deep sense of dread coming over me as we sped along in the car, imagining the worst, whatever that might be. I began to pray earnestly in my heart that everything would be all right as the car sped toward the Sterling/Rock Falls hospital. It wasn't far, but it seemed like a long, long ride.

When we got there I was taken to a special, private waiting room. I knew this was a bad sign. When I walked in there was the doctor, the coroner, my wife and her parents. I remember wondering why my in-laws would be there and how they got here so fast. I remember very clearly the doctor saying something like we did all we could do. I thought, what do you mean we did all we could do? I thought, what did you do and who did you do it to?

It's been a while now since it happened, my summer of paintless everything. As I think about it I'm not sure I was able to go through that summer even remembering I had toes, let alone whether or not they were painted. As I am writing this account I realize this is his birthday week. Today is May 22nd. He died thirty-four years ago today. Thirty-four years is a long time. A lot of the details are fuzzy now. I've lost some hair and not a few brain molecules since then. Plus, there's all the hard knocks that have happened along the way which have rearranged some pieces of the picture. What once resembled a Van Gogh in my mind has now come to look more like a Picasso. Still the parts are painful to recall, even at this distance and with the perspective I now have.

I remember Lora looking at me and saying, "Sam, he's gone." Gone where I thought? And where are Kimberly and Cameron? It began to sink in. He was gone. Forever gone. Dead. A parent's worst nightmare come true. At that point everything went into slow motion. I wondered now what do I do? What do I think and say in a moment like this? What am I supposed to be like? How, as one who has trusted God for everything, am I supposed to act? What do I do? What does a man of faith do when the most precious thing he has is suddenly ripped from his life? Under great pressure who you are comes out. What happens is your default character kicks in. You do what you have been trained to do. You think, say, and believe what you have practiced all of your life before and up until this moment.

Fortunately, I had been raised in a Christian home. I had been given deep values by Christian parents. The book that contained the lives, teachings and writings of more than forty men and women who were so strong, so powerful, so courageous because of their faith in God, the foundational teaching of that book kicked in. I would trust God, because that's what I had been taught to do.

As it would turn out, Kit's death was the beginning of the end, for our marriage, the start of a downhill slide that would lead to even more losses.

I remember the coroner came in, said he had examined the situation and determined it to be an accident. Evidently Lora had put Kit in the tub, with only a small amount of water to splash in, and then went to the other room to put Kimberly and Cameron down for a nap. She said it felt like she was just gone for a moment. When she came back he was laying face down in the inch of water, his lips already turning blue. A small bruise on his temple told the story. He must have tried to crawl out of the tub to follow his mother and fell back in, hitting his head and falling face down. Face up, face down, a small turn would have saved his life.

# PRAYING IN THE EMERGENCY ROOM

After they explained what they felt must have happened to Kit, we were ushered into the emergency room for a moment with our baby. Curtains were pulled all around and workers conspicuously absent. A sheet was pulled to his chin, over his already bloating tummy. His blond hair looked the same, as if he were alive, but his blue eyes were still. They did not turn to meet mine when I entered. The normally busy little boy was lying so still.

I have prayed for the dead a few times in my life, this was the second. I laid my hand on his chest and mustered what little strength I had left and prayed a shaky prayer, with as much faith as I could muster within my aching chest. I don't know what it sounded like to the other people standing there with me, perhaps the last grasping of hope from a father who would soon have to let go, but for me it was different. It was a defining moment that has never left me. I prayed in faith, to a God who I fully believed was able to raise my son from the dead. Like Abraham, I refused to believe that death was the end. I knew his life would go on, whether he got up from the table or not. I have never stopped believing.

# BACK HOME IN PEORIA

The funeral was just a few days later back in Peoria. It was held in a brand new state of the art facility the owners were very proud of. My in-laws were well known in the city and with family, church, my ministry work and friends, the turnout was huge. People were lined up way back out of the viewing room through the funeral home and out into the parking lot. They thought they had made a mistake and built their new facility too small. It took a long time for people to arrive at the small, open casket.

My blond haired little boy was very fond of a kid's tape I had made featuring one of my puppet characters, Special Agent Ralph, and he held it in his hand as people passed along to say goodbye to a little tot who had barely had time to live.

I remember one lady filing past the casket in tears saying, "I'm going to have our swimming pool dug up!" I said, "No, don't do that. God is able to protect your children. They will live every day He has designed for them. And if they go home before you do God will give you the strength to endure."

During that visitation at the funeral home God gave us supernatural strength and we found ourselves comforting others as much or more than they were us. In the days after that God gave us unusual, supernatural strength. Someone said, "You're strong right now because you're in shock," as if to say that was God's way of helping us through the catastrophe. I knew in my heart they were wrong. I knew the presence of God enough to know He was helping me, even though I did not understand why He had let this happen.

In the limo on the way to the cemetery my little Kimberly sat on my lap. She looked up at me and asked, "Are we going to bury Kit?" In that moment the Holy Spirit gave me words of wisdom to say to a five-year old. I said, "No. Just his body. The real Kit left his body and went to Heaven to be with Jesus. He is there and Jesus is responsible to take care of him. It's just that his body was left here and it is our responsibility to take care of that."

I remember crying myself to sleep many nights as the days following the funeral crept by, wondering if he was crying as much for me as I was for him.

Sometime later I was going somewhere with a friend who took it upon himself to make sure I had my theology straight by explaining to me that Satan had made this happen and not God. I thought that means Satan can do whatever he wants in my life. I retorted, "God is in charge of my life! Not Satan! Satan does not own me. God owns me. Jesus is my Lord! He can do what he wants. Satan cannot." My upbringing, all those years I had spent in the word as a child in church, and in a home where I saw believing parents act out before me what I heard taught in church, had planted a deep faith in me that could not be shaken. It kept me going that summer of missing toes.

## GOD ANSWERS WITH A VISION OF COMFORT

A few days after the funeral I remember sitting up in bed one morning wondering who would be there with him in that lonely cemetery and who would take him his bottle, change his diapers and care for him. As I sat weeping a vision took place. I think it was in my heart and mind, but it was so powerful it took over and the room disappeared before my eyes. I saw a picture open up before me, only it was covered by a foggy veil. Then it was like someone was pulling back the curtains. Before me I was looking over Kit's shoulders, across a river toward a glorious city.

On the other bank was a large crowd of people looking back across at us. It was family and friends who had gone on before. They were waiting there on the other side of the river, waiting for Kit to cross over to the other side. They were there to welcome him, to keep him from feeling lost and alone. Among them was Jesus, who I knew would care for him, and would be his daddy and father him into all he was destined to be.

When the picture faded from in front of my eyes my soul was comforted and a deep peace settled onto me. I rested my way through many days of sorrow after that, the vision feeding my need to know Kit was not alone, weeping, but comforted, aching, yet strengthened.

So began the worst summer of my life, a summer of paintless toenails to be sure. I had to go on tour and often tears would be streaming down my cheeks backstage as audiences were laughing at my shows out front.

In retrospect, it was also one of the best summers of my life for it was during that time the Holy Spirit drove faith and hope deep into my heart as I lay crushed before him. It was his personal gift to my broken heart which continues to serve me to this very moment as I write these lines today, thirty-five years later, to this very day.

# The Rest of the Story

Resting in the middle of a storm is hard to do, yet that's exactly what Jesus did. The twelve disciples were with him on the Sea of Galilee when they were engulfed by a terrible, fierce storm. What was Jesus doing? He was sleeping on the bottom of the boat, and he was teaching his disciples a lesson. How could He rest in the middle of the gale force winds? I believe it was because He was absolutely sure about who He was. He was His Father's son, and He

knew His Father had it all under control. You and I are often not so sure, but nevertheless, His Father is our Father and He loves us as much as He loved Jesus. Over time we can choose to build relationship with the Father and the more we know Him, the more we will see who we are in Christ, and that our Father can be trusted, both in the time of rest, and in the stormy time of unrest.

*"Find rest O my soul, in God alone; my hope comes from him."*
PSALMS 62:5 (NIV)

*Sam's To Do List* ———————➤

- ☑ Pick up Some Lunch Meat
- ☑ Plan Funeral
- ☑ Play in Yard with Kids
- ☑ Lay on the Bed and Cry
- ☑ Pay the Mortuary
- ☑ Put one Foot in Front of the Other

## I RESTED MY WAY THROUGH MANY DAYS OF SORROW ...

# Chapter Four

# A Walton's Family Rerun

## SAM

*Shortly* after my son's death I went back to my parent's home with my two surviving kids, Kimberly and Cameron. I intended to stay for six months. I ended up staying six years. It was a healing time for me and my children. The memories of a good childhood, the disciplines and love of a time gone by healed my soul and saved my children.

## COFFEE IN THE SAUCER

Some of my fondest memories come from around the old oak kitchen table at which my family shared meals or played games on snowy winter days when I was growing up. It was brought from Inny Davenport's house across the road when she had passed away and it was at that table that many memories were poured into my heart over the years. It was here that I sat with my mom and dad for seven years before my brothers and sister came along and sat in the same high chair that I had used. Decades later, when I was a full grown man, I sat again at this same table with my own children, where the bountiful banquet of old fashioned cooking filled my empty stomach and the banter of our loving family filled the empty place in my heart when I had lost my wife and youngest son.

When I was little, Grandpa would come in from working on the farm for a noon meal of fried potatoes, sausage, corn on the cob and green beans. Of course there was always a strawberry or pumpkin pie and no meal was complete without a cup of hot steaming coffee fresh roasted in an old fashioned percolator on the top of the coal-burning stove. During the heavy work seasons, when it was time for planting in the spring or harvest in fall, the meals had to be quick, but still there was always the cup of hot steaming coffee.

Mom would pour and then Granpa would add enough sugar to support a whole ant hill or send a perfectly calm child to removing the wallpaper on at least three rooms. He would stir for a bit and then tap the spoon on the edge of the rim and lift the hot steaming cup, not to his lips, but to pour onto the saucer. He would blow on the coffee as he poured and then pour from the saucer back to the cup and never spill a drop. Back and forth he would pour and blow until the steam began to fade. Then he would sip the coffee, often right from the saucer, that had been cooled just right by his perfected method, accumulated from many years of coffee pouring. He knew just when he could sip and his lips were protected from burn by his cup to saucer back and forth pouring technique.

Time has gone by, but I can still see mom's cookies or a cherry pie sitting on the table's red and white checked oilcloth, ready to satisfy the need for a quick pick-me-up morsel for those who pass by. I can still see grandpa Sam Ramseyer sitting at the table, on one of the matching old oak chairs, in his overalls and white hair, pouring his coffee back and forth from here to there and back from there to here again and I realize how much that table brought to our lives. It's where we poured out our hurts and our dreams, back and forth into each other, until they came of age, just right to be tasted and perfect for partaking.

Granpa has long since passed on and we have all long grown up and hurried out the door, just like he did on those busy harvest days. But I'll always remember his pouring and sipping and be grateful for the love we poured into each other while eating together at that old kitchen table that was bought from Inny's house across the road when I was just a little boy.[1]

# GOING BACK HOME

Going home to live again made me feel like a failure. So many hopes and dreams from that kitchen table were shattered. I went home broke and broken after struggling for six years to make a go of it with my first wife. That was about thirty-five years ago as of this writing.

Today they call kids who go back home boomerang kids. In 2012, 36% of the nation's young adults ages 18 to 31—the so-called Millennial generation—were living in their parents' home, according to a new Pew Research Center analysis of U.S. Census Bureau data. This is the highest share in at least four decades and represents a slow but steady increase over the 32% of their same-aged counterparts who were living at home prior to the recession in 2007 and the 34% doing so when it officially ended in 2009.[2]

Kids have been going back home since the beginning of time. Parents, grandparents, kids and grandchildren all living in the same house at the same time is nothing new. In many cultures today, extended family living together is a sign of wealth and a matter of pride. For me going back was a result of failure, but going back home was one of the best things I ever did.

Unfortunately, many kids come back home in this day and age because they've gotten caught up in the drug culture and can't find work or cope with life. Many come home with children they can't support or care for. For me and my kids, going back home was like revisiting the Walton family. It saved our lives.

The Walton's TV show is an American television series that ran for nine seasons beginning back in 1972, starring Ralph Waite, Michael Learned and Richard Thomas. It was about the Walton family, John and Olivia, and their seven children and their elderly parents, Zeb and Esther, who all lived together on Walton's Mountain, West Virginia.

The story is centered on John-Boy, who was the oldest of the children and often narrated the story. The family ekes out a living running a small lumber mill and by doing some small-scale farming. They share hospitality with relatives and strangers alike inviting them in for coffee and pie, just like we used to do around our kitchen table.

The show is centered around familiar town folks. Everyone knew everyone's name and all the history to go with them. All friends and strangers alike who pass by Walton's Mountain get the same good old country hospitality. In the signature scene that closed each episode you see the family house as lights go out in the late evening and you hear everyone bid each other goodnight.

# ROOTS

Our house was the Indiana version of the Waltons'. The land has been in the family for more than five generations. When I arrived my children made the third time four generations had lived together in the farmhouse in its lifetime. My great-grandmother, the fifth generation, lived in the house next to us when I was growing up. Stella connected me to all the things from the first half of the century and her memories became mine. When I returned with my children I was able to walk across our yard and recite for them things that had happened in that spot three decades before, when I was a child.

Meaningful events that become long term memories are emotional stakes in the ground that anchor our children's lives. As grandparents one of the great things you can do that will save your grandchildren is to recite the family history. It will give them a sense of belonging and identity.

I recently saw an ad on TV where you can research your ancestry. The smiling young lady who had found out she was 36% British, 23% Irish, and other percent's of this and that, happily proclaimed, "Now I know who I am." Many children today don't have the roots that can help them become something more than what someone is offering on a street corner. When you share your memories, your past becomes theirs and they find a stable identity that's hard for the street corner drug salesman to beat. Nothing will help your grandchildren truly know who they are like your stories from the good old days about where you grew up, what your parents did and when and how they did it. Your grandkids will draw a great deal of identity from your past.

# A 37 CHEVY MAKES A GREAT MEMORY

My grandfather left me a 1937 Chevy. When I went and pulled it out and dusted it off it was still in pretty good shape. I opened the glove box and found papers grandpa Sam had written on, a  pipe he had smoked and something I never thought, a hand gun! I had no idea he'd ever had one. I had ridden in that car many times as a kid and never seen it. We always discover good and interesting things about who we are when we can open up an old glove compartment somewhere in the recesses of our minds and rediscover who we are by reliving a moment of our past. We need to do this because our past can build their future.

## MAKE MEMORIES BY SHARING MEMORIES

Memories are stored and become part of a child's identity, even if they are just stories you share. Get a journal and jot down ideas about things you have seen or done. Turn off the TV. If you don't share your life, they will get someone else's life, usually fiction from the TV or a video game. Can you imagine your best childhood memory being a video game?

Debbie's kids lit up when they heard their grandpa Otis "Tink" Hale had once fielded a groundball hit by Babe Ruth while playing for the St. Louis Browns. Who knew?! They would never have known if the story hadn't been told. Now they tell the story. It's part of who they are.

My kids heard story after story about what Grandpa Ramseyer did right there on that land we were now living on. Kids today are so transient, not only by moving from place to place, but with families breaking up and new families being formed, their memories are filled more with drama than with events that leave them feeling good about who they are. Heritage builds a child. Share yours and you become part of them. If you don't share yours the drug salesman will sell them one.

**KIDS FIND THEIR LIFE IN THE STORIES YOU TELL ABOUT YOUR LIFE**

# HERE'S MUD IN YOUR EYE

All the kids saw was an old silver pole building. It came alive when I shared how I had helped their great-grandpa Sam Ramseyer build that building way back in 1958. I showed them some of his writing on a post and told them how he and I would take a nap on sacks of grain in an old wagon on a rainy day. I told them how once he called me over to look down in a post hole he was digging and how when I looked down into the hole he dropped the post in and splashed me with muddy water. They laughed when I told how he had laughed and laughed at the look of surprise on my mud covered face. His laughter became mine and mine became theirs. Kids find their life in the stories you tell about your life. Tell them a lot of your stories.

As much as your budget will allow, do things with your grandkids: take in a ball game, go swimming, or to the park, playgrounds, or the lake. Take hikes, bike rides and car day trips. Do anything you can think of. See places, talk about family and history. We raise kids with show and tell. Show them places, tell them stories. Make memories on purpose. Good, positive, laughter filled memories can save your grandchild, and impact generations you will never meet. That's why keeping a journal of your memories makes so much sense.

# THE POWER OF EXTENDED FAMILY

When I arrived back home I was lucky enough to have a brother, Sid, and my sister Susan, who were in their early twenties, and still living at home. They helped save my kids. They helped me care for my kids when I was an emotional wreck. They took care of them while I went to work. It bought me the time I needed to get back on my feet. Brothers and sisters can be a lifesaver, too!

Kids pick up character traits from all the people they spend time with. Extended family members become de facto character DNA simply by being with them. They soak up who you are, so give them time to marinate in your stories, and your laughter. Do crazy things. Roll with them on the yard, pull them into the shower with your clothes on. Play lots of games. We love to play hide and seek in our big house.

Caring for the next generation can provide the older generation purpose that will not only save the lives of the kids, but extend their own lives in the process. People with purpose live longer.

Save your grandkids lives by making them part of a great extended family unit.

# THE BENEFIT OF STRUCTURE

When I arrived home I was beat up and wore down. Life had been so liquid, unpredictable and out of control in the months before going home. When I arrived we had five adults and two kids all using the same small bathroom, so we had to have a schedule. Also, mom's health wasn't good at the time, so added to all the cooking and cozy bathing, everything had to be orderly, predictable and quiet. The tight schedule made life stable again. It was clear what had to be done, and when it had to be done. Children pull stability from a clear, disciplined schedule. The effect is; I am a person who gets up at seven, eats breakfast at eight, goes to day care until noon, eats lunch at noon, goes to Grandma's house in the afternoon, eats dinner at five thirty, plays games with grandpa and grandma until eight, takes my bath at eight-thirty and goes to bed at nine, and to sleep after prayers. The schedule becomes who they are.

You can save your grandchild by providing a clear, structured daily schedule.

# *The Rest of the Story*

Four point nine million American children are being raised solely by their grandparents.[3] It is a calling. It is a special purpose. Bring your grandkids back home, make them sit through some Walton's Mountain reruns and give them a rerun of your own. It will save their lives, as it did ours.

*"And the LORD gave them rest round about,*
*according to all that he sware unto their fathers."*
JOSHUA 21:44 (KJV)

## ENDNOTES

1. *Coffee in the Saucer,* a reading from *Trips Down Memory Lane* by Samuel Lee Bowman, available on amazon.com.
2. http://www.pewsocialtrends.org/2013/08/01/a-rising-share-of-young-adults-live-in-their-parents-home/.
3. USAToday.com, USA Today News, July 27th, 2014, based on U.S. census data, 2010.

Sam's To Do List ————→

- ☑ Pay Some Bills
- ☑ Watch a Walton's Rerun
- ☑ Thank God for My Family
- ☑ Play Hide and Seek

# Chapter Five

# Into the Blender

••• ❦ •••

## SAM
### SEVEN FAMILIES, BUT WHO'S COUNTING?

*Combined,* Debbie and I have had five children and so far we've lost two of them. Two kids in heaven, three to go. Not exactly the way we'd planned, but Heaven is our ultimate objective for our kids and the generations after them.

As of right now Debbie and I have seven grandchildren and four great-grandchildren. Debbie is sixty-two, and in fabulous shape, so she will see many generations after her. (Don't tell Debbie I told you this, but she was a grandmother when she was just thirty-four and a great-grandmother when she was fifty-three). If it wasn't for her premature white hair I swear she would look thirty-five forever. Eat your heart out guys. You should be so lucky at sixty plus.

Together we have been part of seven distinct family units. That's a lot of family. See if you can follow. You might want to fill out one of those baseball score sheets to keep track of all this. Our family tree is so heavy with branches it looks like one of those pine trees full of ice drooping all the way down on the ground, with a tree or two all its own growing out the side.

Debbie grew up in the city with three sisters. I grew up in the country with two brothers and a sister. So far, that's two family units, one each.

Then Debbie got married to Tom and had Stacy and Zachary. I got married to Lora and had three kids: Kimberly, Cameron and Christopher. That makes four families experienced.

When Tom died Debbie was single for a year, just her and the kids. After Kit died and I was divorced, Kim, Cam and I went back home to live with mom and dad and my sister Susan and brother Sid (both adults). In total that made five adults and two kids in four bed rooms and one bathroom. If you're keeping score on your card that's a double, followed by an error, with a stolen base, a walk and one run in. Never mind. So far that's six family units; two each growing up, two each married, two each as single parents.

Next Debbie and I married combining Stacy, Zachary, Kimberly and Cameron, and we don't count Daisy the dog who came along with Debbie. Whew! Now that we've got all that straight . . . well, we at least we have it on paper so it's public record.

There are several stories wound into this blending of so many family histories. In this yours, mine and ours there's merging families, raising each other's kids, helping kids survive a parent's death, grandparents saving grandkids, blending two careers and moving to the country. Also, changing schools, and there is lots more, but we'll save all of that for another chapter, or maybe another book, or maybe a series of books, or maybe a library! Ok, so let's go on with this awesome story of God's redeeming love, working in two families.

# SO HOW DID YOU GUYS MEET ANYWAY?

When you get together with a couple for the first time, what's the question you always ask? "So, how did you guys meet anyway?" First date stories are always fun to hear. Here's ours. Debbie will tell her story first.

## DEBBIE
### DEBBIE'S DOOR

So, here I was, a widow at thirty-two. Something I hadn't planned on. The last couple of years Tom was extensively incapacitated. When he passed he left a big hole in my life, in my heart, and most certainly in my daily routine. I knew I wanted to be married. I wanted a husband, but I definitely did not want to do the dating scene. I wanted God to choose; who, when, and even if, if that's what He wanted for me. I can't control things anyway so why not give the control to One who knows. So I looked up. That's what He had told me to do. I looked up to Heaven and said, "Lord, if you want me to have a husband, you'll have to bring him to my front door." That was it. Simple.

I never went to the door and looked at the back side wondering when or if it would open and who might be on the other side. I trusted God. He had seen me through thus far, so He could plan my future and bring someone to my door, made just for me. Anyway, I was very busy with a full time career, raising two children by myself and adjusting to life without Tom to think anything about husband hunting. Still the nights were lonely and I often cried myself to sleep over my emptiness and where my life would go. Where do you sleep on a bed that once had space reserved for your mate, your lover, the other half of your life? When I prayed the prayer for God to bring me a husband I didn't have any specific expectations. I just wanted a man that loved God. I would get that and a whole lot more I never bargained for. That's the great thing about God. When you give something to Him, He'll always make the best choice, even if it stretches you some.

# SAM
## ON CRUISING FUNERAL HOMES

I'm not sure whether to share my side of the story tongue in cheek, or just stay with the facts. I love a fun story so here goes with the tongue in cheek version. It's the version I tell when someone asks us how we got together. I just say it plain and simple; I went funeral home hopping. It's a great way to meet women. Hey, when you look like I look you have to do what you have to do, right?

Debbie and I often have a great laugh with our friends over my version of our story. Tom had a great sense of humor and we know if he can hear or see us from Heaven he's laughing with us. While my version makes people laugh, Debbie's side of the story inspires people because it reveals the love and favor of God for widows and mothers who trust Him.

I had been single eight years and dated very little. I knew I wanted a woman who loved God, who could help me raise my children to love and fear God. And, after the blender I'd already been through I really didn't want to play the dating scene. I just wanted a little less drama, to love my children and keep my business going.

The very first time I ever saw Debbie it was several years before we ever met. She came into a Sunday school class at Morning Star Church, with Tom hobbling slowly beside her on a cane. I saw a man struggling along, slow, dragging steps, and a wonderful wife at his side helping him along. I thought, "There's the kind of woman I'd like. Lucky guy."

As Tom became more sick over time the whole church was drawn into praying for his healing, his children and Debbie. The dying person suffers, but the mate suffers, too. We all knew it was a tough situation, pulling hard on all involved. Along with many others I visited Tom, gave him cards and encouragement, and a few badly needed laughs.

I remember seeing Debbie in the shadows, but she managed to stay pretty much in the background. In all those visits to their house I don't remember ever saying a word to Debbie. I didn't give her much thought other than to admire, at a distance, the way she was caring for her husband, keeping a full time job going and watching over her children.

The very first words I ever said to Debbie were at Tom's funeral. I waited in line wondering what I should say to a grieving widow I didn't even know. When it was my turn I stepped up to the casket and looked her right in her eyes for the very first time. I think I said something like, "Debbie, I am so sorry." She was saying something back while I was thinking, *"Wow, this is a good looking woman."* [mentally slap myself in the face, what?! Stop that.] She said something back to me. I don't remember what. I do remember what I was thinking, *"This is one fine woman. I wonder how long I should wait before I ask her out? I'll wait one year"* I thought. [mental self-head-butt! Sam get ahold of yourself.] I know my ears were on and my mouth was moving, but what my brain was saying was, *"What if someone beats me to it? How could I possibly compete with the men that will come courting this fine lady?"* [Ahhhhhh! How can you think this at a time like this? You have got to be kidding.] I gave her the obligatory hug, turned and walked on into the waiting area wondering who that was that had just had that mental conversation with himself at the funeral of a friend.

I looked at my watch. Three hundred sixty-five days, twenty-three hours, fifty-nine minutes and thirty seconds before I can dial her phone. I had never seen a second hand moving slower. But, God had other plans. He was going to work a little quicker than I thought.

## DEBBIE IS WATCHING AND SO IS GOD

I had watched Sam at a distance. When I first saw him he was worship leader at Christian Life Fellowship. I loved the way this single father was caring for his children and I admired his commitment to the Lord. Then two years or so later I opened the front door to see who was there and there he was. Sam, holding a dish of baked beans. I smiled and invited him in.

Pastor Logan Sparling had instituted new home groups at the church and he assigned Sam and I to the same group. By "happenchance" the very first time my life support group met was at my house. So, God, in His own way and timing, sent Sam to my front door.

Our sons, Zachary and Cameron hit it off that night and Zachary wanted to go home with Sam so he could play with Cameron. Sam invited the whole group to come out to see the new house he had just moved into the week before. I was the only one who showed up since I had to go out to get Zachary. We sat and talked at the kitchen table while the boys played. After that we were never really apart. Little did we know, talking over that kitchen table would become the hallmark and center of our marriage.

"I WANT YOU TO LOVE ME. I WANT YOU TO TRUST ME ENOUGH TO LET ME LOVE YOU, AND I WANT YOU TO STAY HERE WITH ME SO WE CAN BUILD A LIFE TOGETHER."

*Michael to Sarah*
*Francine Rives, Redeeming Love*

## BACK TO SAM

That spring I did what anybody does when it comes time to pop the question; I loaded the potential wife, her kids, my kids, and some other miscellaneous kids and a few pets into a Shasta Motor home and drove 24 hours straight to the Florida Beaches. I figured surviving a week in a little motor home would be a great litmus test for surviving a marriage where two families were going to get thrown into the mixing bowl of life. Turns out I was right, but it wouldn't be easy. Debbie said yes and we were married in June, fourteen months after Tom passed away.

Those were good days and exciting days, some of the best times of my life. It was challenging from the very beginning, blending two families, moving, putting Debbie's kids in a new school, getting our kids all settled in a house we were renovating to make room for this big new family. I had to go out on tour just a month later and we parted at our new front door, the first of many times, as I would continue to tour with the Granpa Cratchet shows for many more years. We were both pretty independent people at that point so being apart actually worked pretty well. I ran the business, Debbie worked and ran the house and we began to tug and pull with each other about how to raise each other's kids.

## The Rest of the Story

Through it all God gave us a rest. We never doubted that putting our lives together had been the right thing to do. Debbie and I were M.F.E.O. (Made For Each Other) The kids didn't always think so, but there can be rest in the midst of chaos, and plenty of that there would be, both rest and chaos.

*"There remaineth therefore a rest to the people of God."*
HEBREWS 4:9 (KJV)

## Sam & Debbie's To Do List ——✧

- ☑ Make Kids Get Along (Sam & Debbie)
- ☑ Mow the Yard (Sam & Cameron)
- ☑ Move Debbie's Kids to New School (Debbie, Zachary & Stacy)
- ☑ Short Honeymoon to Brown County (Sam & Debbie)
- ☑ Move Boxes from Debbie's House to Country House (Sam, Cameron, Zachary, Debbie & Stacy)
- ☑ Spend Time in the Word (Sam & Debbie)

## Chapter Six

# *In Sickness and In Health*

--- ···✦∘✦··· ---

## DEBBIE

*In* sickness and in health, for better or for worse, till death do us part. They don't say those words much anymore. Vows aren't said that much these days and if they are people don't include a lot of those deep value sayings that really make life work. When Sam and I went to the altar we said till death do us part, and we meant it. This level of commitment forced us to come to the kitchen table and talk things out, to solve our problems, to make things work. We figure if we were stuck with each other why not make it a good kind of stuck?

One-part communication, one-part humility, a heaping dose of forgiveness, one-part willingness to hear the other person out, one-part freedom to say totally what's on one's mind and you have a recipe for marital survival and a foundation on which to build a great marriage. Ours was about to take a hit.

# FOR BETTER OR FOR WORSE

A "for worse" came to Sam and I in the summer of 1999. We had been married eleven years at this point and we had already been through a lot with the kids. I got up early and went in to work at three a.m. on a Monday for a twelve-hour shift in the intensive care unit. Through the day I became tired and began to have double vision. I got dizzy and I lost any sense of balance. My left eye turned all the way to the inside like it was dead. I had to stop working.

Doctors sent me to a room where I took off my scrubs and stopped being a nurse, put on a nightgown and became a patient. Just like that, in a matter of minutes a long rewarding career was over. Without my balance and eyesight I couldn't continue to do the intricate work nursing called for. I wouldn't be able to do anything at all for that matter. Basic movement across a room became nearly impossible.

I went through all the tests I was used to administering to others. They did an MRI, blood work and my husband held my hand while they did a spinal tap. X-rays showed lesions in my brain and the tap showed oligo clonal bands, both usual signs of M.S. I thought not again. My first husband had died of M.S., my sister Marcie was debilitated by M.S., and now I had it. Strike three.

They put me on heavy steroids while I was there and suggested all kinds of medications, all the while making sure we knew nothing would fix it, and there would be no guarantees for the future. We prayed together and committed the situation to the Lord.

After losing my husband, and Sam losing a child, we knew there were no guarantees in life, that anything can happen at any time. He and I live our days like there may be no tomorrow, as if every time we part we may never see each other again. It's a good way to live. It keeps life and each other in high value.

# SAM
## DRAW ON YOUR FAITH ACCOUNT

It's a poor thing to start saving a year before retirement, but many people never store up faith, or even look for it until after disaster strikes. As much as God hates death, and it breaks His heart to see His precious ones suffer and die[1], without death you and I would never ultimately face the truth. We need Jesus and death sets a deadline. Who will we serve?

It's bad enough to face whatever disaster may show up at your door without a bank account filled with money, let alone have disaster come knocking and find your faith account empty, your soul bankrupt of hope. Many cry out in painful times and that is good. God is always glad to hear from us. He is so patient and gracious to receive us with open arms, even when we have been ignoring Him.

# SAM WELDS HIS WAY TO WISDOM

I remember one time I was welding on a show trailer I had committed to build for my clients. I was worn out, behind schedule, low on funds, stressed out and had gone days without sleep. Exhausted, I was welding along sometime in the middle of the night talking to God about things. I said "God, every time something goes wrong it's always my fault. Everything that has ever gone wrong in my life was always all my fault. It's never your fault. I know that if anything goes wrong for all the rest of my life it will always be my fault. Do you know, God, how hard it is knowing it's always going to be my fault? It will never, ever be your fault. Do you know how hard it is to live with someone who is perfect?" Instantly, the strong voice of the Holy Spirit within me spoke up and said words that are forever branded into my soul, "Yes, my son. I know. That is why I am so patient and gracious with you." My shoulders shook. I sobbed in my welding helmet and I have drawn on those words many times since that night.

## HEARING GOD'S VOICE IS WHAT FILLS YOUR LIFE BANK ACCOUNT WITH FAITH

There is great value in cultivating an ability to hear God's voice. It's what fills your life bank account with faith.[2] Once God speaks, the power of His word cascades forward in your life and it never stops supporting you and feeding you, even when the present situation passes. You can dine out on one word from God for a lifetime, but you often need a fresh word. But, do you choose to spend time dining out on His written word when you have the opportunity, when you still have a choice? Do we invest time in His presence and dialogue with God so our faith accounts will be full when we desperately need to make a withdrawal? Or do we turn on the TV and fill our minds with useless dialogue that fills us with nothing?

In a time of great distress many call out to God, but hear nothing. They mistakenly think God is far away, or is mad at them. The truth is, God is never angry with us. He is not distant. He is not reluctant. It's just that we have not learned to listen, we have not cultivated hearing. We get angry at God because He does not give us what we think He should give, when we think He should give it, in the way we think He should. We are angry with the very One with whom we have spent so little time, and know so little about.

## HEARING FROM GOD IS AN ART FORM

Hearing God is an art form you increase by practice. Just like you learn English, you must take the time to learn the language of God. Just like learning to play an instrument, it takes education, time and practice.[3] Without this process, when the time comes to hear, you will mistakenly think He does not speak.

Our left brains contain reasoning, math, logic, and the ability to see and retain facts. The right brain is art, music, creativity, and intuition. It enables us to take the facts, put them together in creative ways and find new solutions. God gave us both sides. In the left we know God by learning facts about Him. In the right side we can know God by revelation from God. In our western culture version of Christianity we have overused our left side till the right has atrophied. We experience so little of God's power because we are right brain dead. That is why so many other cultures see evidence of God in supernatural occurrences and we see so few. We have been raised in left brained discipline for so long that even when we begin to move to a left/right balance, it seems so out of balance we become afraid to enter in. Jesus said the Holy Spirit would guide us into all truth.[4] Is He not able?

Not many of us know how we could possibly walk into the Whitehouse right now and make demands on the President of the United States. Yet we quickly try to walk into the throne room of an Almighty God without knowledge of how to approach Him. This God who numbers all the atoms in the universe, and keeps every one of them perfectly in place in a hundred billion galaxies, in a universe that's a billion light years across, is far beyond the reach of our puny little left brains, yet there we run in times of pressure, like a flea trying to wake an elephant. Do you think we can casually approach this awesome God without studying His book in order to understand the demands of His presence? You had better believe if we had to appear in the White House next week we would read the book on White House decorum this week!

It takes time, study, meditation and practice to learn how to enter the throne room and make requests of the King. This one thing I can say at this point in my

**GOD IS PLEASED BY AND RESPONDS TO A HEART THAT POSITIONS ITSELF BEFORE HIM IN HUMILITY AND FAITH**

experience; it is better to invest the time to learn how to be close to Him, and how to foster a hearing ear, than to try to run into His presence and get something out of Him by throwing some kind of emotional tantrum in the heat of the crisis. He does not respond to anger. He cannot be controlled. He is pleased by and responds to a heart that positions itself before Him in humility and faith.[5] But, don't be afraid to cry out to Him from whereever you are in your spiritual walk.[6]

That day in the hospital when Debbie had lost part of her sight, we did what we knew would work. We humbled ourselves before God, as we had so many times before. I knew that even if I did not understand Him that I could trust Him. Debbie and I have learned to trust Him only by practicing trust, through many encounters and many situations.

It's never a good idea to try to find oil to fill the storm lamp after the storm has already started. Much of the time we do not understand what He was doing or why, but this we do understand, that He loves us and is faithful to comfort, and to guide, so we practice trusting, which puts us in a position to receive from Him when the storm rolls in.

Even when life is very painful and we lose loved ones like a husband, a father, or a son, we know that if we trust Him, He will either deliver us from the disaster or He will see us through it and heal us when it's over. I know that whatever I lose in the middle of trusting Him, He is faithful to replace, in His own time and in His own way. I have learned that fear, doubt and resentment never move the hand of God. Only steadfast faith moves His heart. Nothing pleases Him more than those whose hearts are broken while they are trusting Him. He rewards those who chose to trust.

As Job said, though you slay me, yet will I serve you. As the three Hebrew children said to King Nebuchadnezzar, we do not know whether God will save us, but if He does not, we will still trust Him and if He does we still will not bow down and worship your false god.

Debbie remembers saying to people, even to her own children as they visited her in the hospital that "God's ways are not our ways." She had a deep peace about the situation. We did not know how this would turn out, but we knew there was no place to hide except in the shelter of the wings of the Almighty. It's a choice. You humble yourself, you bow to Him, you commit your life, whether richer or poorer, in sickness or in health, and for better or worse. When you do He will never fail to draw close to you, teach you, comfort you, give you wisdom for the season and reveal whatever it is you need to know in order to bring you to a place of abundant peace.

Debbie and I prayed together in that hospital room and we practiced what we had practiced so many times before. We ran under the shelter of His wings and great peace flooded over us. We knew that we did not need to know what our future held, because we knew we had committed our lives and our hearts into the hands of the One who held our future. If Debbie never got her eyesight or balance back, we knew God would make a way, and He has.

## ANOTHER MATTER

While Debbie and I rested in great peace her children were another matter. They did not do so well. They were angry and resentful at God over losing their father, the thought of losing their mother was a great burden to them. We did for them what we would do for anyone, we comforted them with our steadfast faith, but neither received it.

To go through life angry at God is worse than sickness to the bones.[13] They cried and fretted. One got angrier and the other turned deeper to medications, both refusing to trust Jesus, who was waiting with arms wide open to love and heal, if they would let Him.

Debbie went back to work with a patch over her left eye, which she wore for about six weeks. One doctor nicknamed her Veggiepatch

## DEBBIE'S PRESCRIPTION FOR NUTRITIONAL HEALING

I have been a lacto-ovo vegetarian since my college days: which means I don't eat meat but I do eat milk, cheese and eggs.

"For many years, researchers have recognized that diets high in fruit, vegetables, and grain, and legumes, appear to reduce the risk of a number of diseases, including cancer, heart disease, diabetes, and high blood pressure when compared with diets high in meat."*

My tip is this: **If you are going to save the next generation you have to take care of yourself.**

*A Prescription for Nutritional Healing by Phyllis A. Balch, p23.

because she was a vegetarian wearing an eye patch. He still calls her that even though the patch is long gone. Debbie's healing was slow. Over the next few weeks her left eye went back to normal. She refused all medical treatment and remains medicine free to this day. Who knows what toll all those medications would have taken on her over all this time.

We are in no way advocating this is what you should do. You must consult your doctor and make your own decision, but Debbie was skeptical because Tom, even though he had M.S., his actual cause of death was complications from being immuno-compromised because of taking all the medication. Debbie chose vitamins, antioxidants, her meatless diet, stress reduction and prayer as her method of treatment.

As Debbie says, "I am in Father God's hands and I cast all my cares on Him for He cares for me." She said what Tom said, "Whichever way it goes I get totally healed."

Whatever happens you can rest assured that God cares for you too. Whatever situation you find yourself in turn to Him, trust in Him. Give you heart and life to Him. It's the only way to live and it's the only way to die. It is now seventeen years later. Debbie has completed forty years of intensive care nursing, healthy as ever.

## The Rest of the Story

His rest never fails to come upon us when we relinquish the problem to Him. Will we still have to face the music? Perhaps. Will we still have to pay the price for our mistakes? Maybe. But I know this, as I love Him hope comes, because I know there is always a way, even if I cannot see it, or understand it. When you come to know that He is indeed the God of the impossible, that an answer can come from nowhere in a flash, you begin  to rest, for you know, that whatever you're facing, this too shall pass.[14]

*"May your unfailing love rest upon us, O*
*Lord, even as we put our hope in you."*
PSALMS 33:22 (NIV)

# ENDNOTES

1. Psalms 116:15 "Precious in the sight of the LORD is the death of his saints" (KJV).
2. Romans 10:17 "Faith comes to us when we hear God's voice speak to us" (Sam's version).
3. *4 Keys to Hearing God's Voice*, by Dr. Mark Virkler, available on amazon.com and online at Christian Leadership University.
4. John 16:13 "Howbeit when he, the Spirit of truth, is come, he will guide you into all truth."
5. I Peter 5:6 "Humble yourself under the mighty hand of God and He will exalt you in due time" (Sam's version).
6. I John 3:1 KJV.
7. Matthew 25:1-12 The parable of the virgins who ran out of oil.
8. Matthew 7:24, 25 "Therefore whosoever heareth these sayings of mine, and doeth them, I will liken him unto a wise man, which built his house upon a rock: And the rain descended, and the floods came, and the winds blew, and beat upon that house; and it fell not: for it was founded upon a rock."
9. Psalms 66:12 "Thou hast caused men to ride over our heads; we went through fire and through water: but thou broughtest us out into a wealthy place."
10. Isaiah 61:7 "For your shame you shall have double; and for your confusion they shall rejoice in their portion: there in their land they shall possess the double: everlasting joy shall be upon them."
11. Job 13:15.
12. Daniel 3:17, 18.
13. Proverbs 17:22 "A merry heart doeth good like a medicine: but a broken spirit drieth the bones."
14. Deuteronomy 28:1 and 28:15 "It shall come to pass . . ." used out of context to say all things that come to us eventually will pass. However, the context of these two references talk specifically about what we get or don't get when we hear God's voice.
15. *Failing Forward* by John Maxwell available on Amazon.com.

# Sam & Debbie's To Do List

- ☑ Spend Time in Meditation on the Word and in Prayer
- ☑ Pick up Some Bananas
- ☑ Read Another Chapter in *Failing Forward* by John Maxwell[15]
- ☑ Tell my Wife I Will Love Her, No Matter What ... Until the Day I Die
- ☑ Wash the Front Windows
- ☑ Take Dad to Lunch

WE RAN UNDER THE
SHELTER OF HIS WINGS
AND GREAT PEACE
FLOODED OVER US

## Chapter Seven

# The Life We Choose

····⚜····

## DEBBIE

*Zachary* came into the world in the most wonderful way. He was born on the perfect day, Valentine's day. What better way to make a mom's heart sing than to birth her baby on that special day of love. He was a challenge, but I loved him through thick and thin, no matter what.

Any child is such a complex menagerie of nature and nurture that it makes it impossible to extract a formula that will guarantee they turn out healthy and productive. However, mothers and awesome grandmothers alike care about the outcome and we can band together, share our failures, successes, ideas, insights and help one another have a greater chance for success.

We must have a clear vision of where we want to take our children, and carry through with much prayer and involvement. If I share some of my story, maybe that will help you share your story. I think you'll find we all have much in common, we're fighting for the lives of a generation.

We need to get things out in the open, so I'll summarize Zachary's life and along the way share some awesome grandparent principles. We'll also be sharing some research and insights from other writers on the subject of raising kids and grandkids. We're not writing a volume about child-rearing, there are already a lot of good resources out there. What we are going to do here is look at some of the important components of our son's life and see what we can extract that might help you.

Zachary had a kind heart and a great smile. He was likeable and loved by many. However, as early as thirteen he started running with the wrong crowd and got into drugs. Even though we are sure he gave his heart to Jesus while at New Creations home for teens, he just couldn't overcome the addictions.

AWESOME GRANDPARENTING PRINCIPLE: I WILL MEET TOGETHER REGULARLY WITH OTHER GRANDPARENTS FOR ENCOURAGEMENT AND INSIGHTS

The auto accident that took his life was do, at least in part, to the multiple drugs they found in his system. We did everything we knew to do, but perhaps we didn't let him do the one thing we should have very early on; let him take the brunt of his decisions. Instead we bailed him out many times and sheltered him from the consequences of his behavior.

If you have been in, are presently in, or think you are headed toward Zachary's scenario then let me say a word just for you, there is rest and hope at the foot of the cross. We made it through, so can you. We are determined more than ever to save the next generation, without the mistakes we made with the last. To that end we hope what we share here will help turn the tide in your situation, heal your heart and give you hope for the future.

Here are four components, or influences we want to talk about in this chapter:

1. DNA

2. Personality

3. Family

4. Special events

# DNA
## (DEFECTIVE BUT NON-NEGOTIABLE ATTRIBUTES)

Some things about our children are built into their DNA. We dream of a quiet, wonderfully peaceful, always happy and smiling child who is ever compliant, and fulfills our every need for love and acceptance. Instead what we get is a child that runs the house from six am to midnight, loves to race motor bikes into big piles of mud, then drag it all through the front door, who loves to swing from the chandeliers every time we turn our back for a second and could care less about our delicate feelings.

Nature gives our children attributes from generations before. Back just five generations DNA comes from a mix of sixty-four people. Most of the time you can see the personality developing right from birth.

# PERSONALITY

Zachary's personality was obvious right away. He was outgoing, energetic and strong-willed. The importance of recognizing your child's personality is vital. Any personality can take a person down any path and a certain type doesn't guarantee a certain outcome. However, caregivers need to adjust their approach to the child's personality and tailor responses in every area; discipline, motivating, correcting, communicating and so

AWESOME GRANDPARENTING PRINCIPLE: RECOGNIZE MY GRANDCHILD'S UNIQUE PERSONALITY AND TAILOR MY PARENTING STYLE ACCORDINGLY

on, according to the needs and responses of the child's general nature.

Early on Zachary rode his hot wheels right out onto a busy road and didn't even think about it. He once went to a friend's house across the highway without informing me as to his whereabouts and it took me a long time to find him. When I disciplined him he just took it and didn't seem to care. I had him tested in elementary school for ADD. He couldn't seem to focus.

Did Zachary's personality type guarantee he would become an addict or give him a propensity toward that lifestyle? "According to those who subscribe to the theory of addictive personality, there are certain personal characteristics which are found to be more common among addicts. These include compulsive behavior, difficulty in controlling impulses, as well as a propensity for developing physical addiction."[1] Research states that genes are not totally responsible for personality.[2]

So many factors affect the direction of a child's life and create the adult they will become. Research can't tell us the course our child will choose. However, research, personal experience and common sense give us mile posts around which we can gauge the impact events and decisions will make on our children and grandchildren.

In all scenarios, we must fight for our grandchildren and for their futures. We must purposefully look at, evaluate and think about how what we are doing with them every day will instill character, and give them knowledge to face the world and win. Nowadays they must survive an onslaught of media, whose only objective is to own their decision making habits, who have no interest in making sure your grandchild has a good future.

# FAMILY

When Zachary was a toddler Tom was just beginning to get sick and became preoccupied with his illness. I (Debbie) was working full time and taking care of Tom, while watching over the kids. It cannot be precisely stated, at this far point in time, whether Zachary got all the personal attention his personality needed. Kids need an abundant amount of your time and attention.

Today many busy parents use the TV, internet and video games to babysit their child. According to BBC news, children age five to sixteen spend an average of six hours in front of a screen each day, compared with around three hours in 1995.[3] Awesome grandparents don't just take kids to activities, they strive to provide generous amounts of time and attention, through daily activities where they are personally involved.

## FAMILY: ROLE EXAMPLES

Something very positive can be said for a child who gets consistent exposure to healthy, Biblical male and female roles over an extended period of time in a stable situation.

Consider these facts:

- Only 46% of US kids younger than 18 are living in a traditional home[4]
- Children of broken homes are more likely to engage in delinquent behavior[5]

- Children from fatherless homes are more likely to be poor, become involved in drug and alcohol abuse, drop out of school, and suffer from health and emotional problems[6]

- 85% of all youths in prison grew up in a fatherless home[7]

Studies make it clear that the effect of a broken home is significant and negative.

In 1950 the average number of single parent homes, or broken homes was only 12 in 100, 8 of those resulting from death and 4 by divorce. By 1992 that figure had grown to 58 in 100, with the death rate remaining at about eight, and the rest being accounted for by divorce and other factors that broke up the home.[8] The emotional consequence of the death of a spouse varies to each child, but it is abundantly clear the impact is significant.

The impact of extended family is huge. Sam went home with his children where his parents, an adult brother and an adult sister were still living at the time. The stability of that family unit saved their lives.

# SPECIAL EVENTS

There are lots of ways to lose a parent; death and divorce are obvious, but anything that robs a child of the nurture of a parent is traumatic and can cause problems later in life: sickness, incarceration, obesity, lengthy time away on business, simply acting cool toward a child, or displaying unpredictable behavior patterns. Anything that causes a parent to be absent in the relationship can have the same effect as death. An absence of good parenting is just as harmful, sometimes more so, than an absent parent. There are over twenty million homeless or abandoned children in the world today – a majority of them are orphans.[9] Perhaps a society that will abandon the unborn eventually comes to abandon those who make it past birth.

Combined with the trauma of Tom's death and hormones my daughter Stacy went into depression and began acting out in her early teens. She is now forty years of age, has settled down, is productive, and is following in my footsteps, working as a nurse. People have commented to us about how good she is with their sick loved ones.

When Zachary became thirteen he began having behavior issues and using in order to self-medicate. In one counseling session he said when I remarried he felt like he lost both parents. During the early days I was dealing with the situation mostly by myself. Looking back, I practiced overcompensation, since the kids lost their dad. I was attempting to create a meaningful connection through spending and spoiling. I have had to deal with the guilt over this by laying it at the foot of the cross.

## The Rest of the Story

No matter what is going on around you, cultivate the art of resting in the midst of the chaos. Take solace in the assurance that if the prodigal is raised in the way of God they will not depart from that way. Pray they will come to their senses as the prodigal son did and return to God, family, and a productive life.[10]

*"And my people shall dwell in a peaceable habitation,*
*and in sure dwellings, and in quiet resting places."*
ISAIAH 32:18 (AMP)

# ENDNOTES

1. Narconon.org, article: *Are Certain Personality Types Prone to Drug Use?*
2. Phychologytoday.com, July 11th, 2013, article: *Do Genes Influence Personality?* by Dr. Michael W. Krause.
3. BBC.com, BBC News, May 27th, 2015 by technology reporter Jane Wakefield.
4. Pewresearch.org, December 22nd, 2014, Pew Research Center.
5. Rebecca Hagelin, *Home Invasion,* page 81, by Nelson Current Publishing, copyright 2005.
6. Fathers.com, National Center for Fathering. Article: *The Consequences of Fatherlessness.*
7. Fathermag.com. Article: *Fatherless Homes Breed Violence.*
8. www.heritage.org article: *How Broken Families Rob Children of Their Chances for Future Prosperity* by Patrick F Fagan, Ph.D.
9. Abandonedchildrensfund.org Article: *Abandoned Children Struggle for Survival.*
10. Luke 15:11-32 The story of the prodigal son.

## Debbie's To Do List ⟶⋆

- ☑ Spend Time in the Word
- ☑ Have Lunch with A Friend
- ☑ Spend Time Around the Kitchen Table with Sam
- ☑ Plant Some Flowers Around the Front Porch

THERE IS REST AND HOPE AT
THE FOOT OF THE CROSS

# Chapter Eight

# The Life We Lose

## SAM

*Let's* continue our look at who and what wants to control your grandchildren with these big five influencers:

1. Drugs

2. Culture

3. Choices

4. Friends & Peer Pressure

5. Media

## DRUGS

The effect of drugs is not limited to the scope of personal use. Tobacco and pot smoke effects anyone living and breathing in the house.[1] Any one person using drugs in the house effects the whole house, including extended family. A casual attitude toward drugs or alcohol in the home will filter into the children's attitude toward drugs and life in general. A culture of drugs will include a whole host of maladies including, but not limited to lying, theatrics, thieving, control, and using people. All these have a huge effect on the children and the grandchildren, and often even to the third and fourth generations.

Grandparents need to know the signs of Drug Addiction:

- Grades falling

- Skipping school

- Closed bedroom door

- On the phone a lot and keeping the phone secret

- Resisting any kind of meaningful conversation

- Doesn't want you to know where they are

- Doesn't want you to know who they are with

- Belligerent attitude

- Discipline problems at school

- Won't complete chores

- Undesirable people coming into the house

- Money missing from your purse or wallet

- Items missing from around the house

When you see any one of these indicators in your child or grandchild's life, plow into their life like a bulldog bulldozer. They need to know you will not put up with it.

## DO NOT PASS GO – DO NOT COLLECT $200
## DO NOT GET OUT OF JAIL FREE

When the children have come to the point where they fail to react to any amount of control or discipline, incarceration becomes the only alternative. Perhaps the hardest thing you will ever do, but the best thing you could do is leave them in county lock up, especially the first time, right up to the time they have to face the judge. When he says they can get out, then they can get out. The local jail will never be as bad as they say as they're crying and pleading for you to get them out. I guarantee it will not be as bad as a state penitentiary will be on down the line. Save them now by leaving them in the system, or you won't be able to save them later. Save your get out of jail free card until later, when they may really need it.

Grandparents must be able to recognize the signs of drug addiction and seek early and radical intervention, no matter how much it hurts. Many of us have made the mistake of assuming the problems are passing, that children will grow out of it, that they're just rough patches, that can be fixed with short term solutions, usually involving spending. In reality, in drug addiction, purchasing what seems to pacify the child at the moment usually backfires, enabling them to manipulate the one with the purse strings and the problem only grows. Seeking short term solutions only masks the problems, when acute intervention is

AWESOME GRANDPARENTING PRINCIPLE: SAVE YOUR GET OUT OF JAIL FREE CARD FOR LATER—LET GRANDKIDS WHO HAVE CHOSEN TO BREAK THE LAW EXPERIENCE THE FULL FORCE OF THE LAW, ESPECIALLY THE FIRST TIME

needed. Many don't see the problems as significant, long term, emotional and mental problems until it's too late.

# CULTURE

Look at how our culture has changed in fifty years. Consider these trends:

1. Increase in drug use

2. Increase in sexual promiscuity

3. Increase in violent crime

4. More parents living together, outside the bonds of marriage

5. Increase in the focus on personal pleasure rather than personal responsibility

6. The replacement of I-take-responsibility with I-have-rights

Something has gone wrong in our culture in just one generation. We thought we were raising our children right, and yet now we a face an epidemic of children who are unable to support their children. What went wrong? Debbie and I sit at the kitchen table and ask ourselves, what did we do wrong and how will we make sure we do not repeat the same mistakes with Zachary's son.

## THE EROSION OF FAMILY

As we consider how to raise the next generation we must also factor in the erosion of family, and the condition of our culture gone stark raving mad. It's the culture our grandchildren will be growing up in, and without a major spiritual change, the culture they will be raising their children in will be even worse. It is so important to learn how to instill a Biblical worldview, for the truths and principles of the Bible are so powerful, universal and time tested we can rest assured they will produce good results for generations to come.[2]

As grandparents we cannot, with these current cultural trends, assume that what we did forty years ago will work with our grandkids today. We must purposefully evaluate our methods. We must band together to create new solutions and to encourage each other to resist the pressure of the pop culture to give in. We must fight for our grandchildren and for a return to a Biblical standard in our culture and in our homes.

We must not only evaluate our methods, but evaluate ourselves. We cannot raise our children to become what we are not. At one point Debbie and I decided two things; 1) it was useless to try to constantly correct our adult kids and, 2) the best thing we could do was simply live the best life in front of them we could, wait for them to see and come asking how we did it. If they can't see, and if they won't ask, you can bet they won't listen anyway. When I say best I don't mean we show them

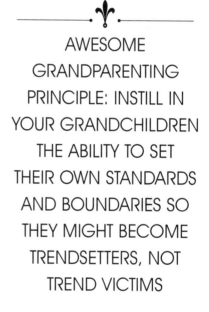

AWESOME GRANDPARENTING PRINCIPLE: INSTILL IN YOUR GRANDCHILDREN THE ABILITY TO SET THEIR OWN STANDARDS AND BOUNDARIES SO THEY MIGHT BECOME TRENDSETTERS, NOT TREND VICTIMS

a bigger house or a newer car. I mean show them the best of loving each other in life and marriage, where we are loving, happy and productive.

## INTENTIONAL GRANDPARENTING

We must live each day, raising our grandkids with intentionality. We must look at and evaluate our daily habits on purpose and to do that our purpose must be clear; give our grandchildren the opportunity to discover and adopt Biblical disciplines that will create in them the ability to set their own standards and boundaries so they might become trendsetters, not trend victims. We cannot just give them rules, we must instill in them the ability to see, think, evaluate and create Biblical worldview answers on their own.

In spite of the mistakes even good parents make, kids can turn out just fine. I know firsthand a situation where the kids were raised in a broken home with an abusive alcoholic father, until he finally disappeared, leaving them in rags with a mom who couldn't find work, and they all became very successful; two executives, one brain surgeon, and all with good families. Others who grow up with good parents may turn out to be addicts and couch surfers.[3] Even so, we cannot take a fatalistic, what-ever-will-be-will-be view. We must raise our grandchildren with intentionality. We must become deeply involved in their daily lives. We must evaluate our parenting skills and never assume our grandchildren will turn out right on their own. If we believe the present world culture will raise our grandkids for us and they turn out well, or as we want them, we are living in La-La Land. Disaster is on the way, again. We're not in Kansas anymore, Toto.

## DEMONS IN THE DETAILS

Looking back after sixty-five years, and seeing all the changes that have come to our society in the last half century, I can confidently say; the demons lie hidden in the details. The contents of one's life soup can be as varied and extensive as the number of ingredients you find in any grocery. The various components come from a wide range of sources; media, school, other parents, peers, DNA, unusual events and personal perception. All play a role, and I'm sure you can name many more.

As much as actual fact, the child's perception of what has happened also plays a role, whether that perception is accurate or not. And then there is the child's free will choice to do what he wants with what he has been given.

# CHOICES

If kids choose drugs they may think it's freedom, but it's really bondage. Drugs greatly cloud reasoning and logic and eyesight.

## WE MUST LET OUR CHILDREN FAIL AND IN DOING SO TEACH THEM HOW TO FAIL FORWARD.

The key is to give the child choices very early, right from the beginning and purposefully let them have the hard knocks of their choices and teach them how to make good choices and how to recover when they fail. We must teach them failure is not fatal. We must let our children fail and in doing so teach them how to fail forward.[4]

Very early on I gave Kimberly and Cameron permission to make their own choices and that I would step in with rules only if they began to make unwise choices. They have not been perfect children, my parenting wasn't perfect either, but it seemed to work well. The point is, letting children have the consequences of bad choices early on, closely monitored by parents, when the choices won't have too great a consequence, is valuable.

The older they get, the bigger the choices, the harder the consequences and the harder it is for you to back off and let them experience those consequences. Worse, we have taught them they can do what they want and expect the bailout. Then when they finally don't get the expected fix all funds, they will get angry with you.

It's a bail out culture we live in. The government bails us out all the time for our poor choices, because we demand it. One day soon we may wake up to find out China owns us and, they will take drastic measures to control us and we will have no one to bail out but ourselves.

———— • ❦ • ————

AWESOME GRANDPARENTING PRINCIPLE: IF YOU REALLY WANT TO KNOW WHAT'S GOING ON WITH YOUR GRANDKID'S FRIENDS, CHECK OUT THEIR FRIEND'S PARENTS

## FRIENDS AND PEER PRESSURE

We all know about peer pressure and how important it is to choose the right friends. You need to become deeply involved in friend choices early on and keep your involvement strong as you slowly transfer the responsibility. Never give up. Never give in. You have the right and the responsibility to know where they are at all times and know who they are hanging with. Start young, stay consistent, so when they are older they will be used to your evaluation and fair judgment. Know that other kids might be fine for your grandchild, but other parents might not have the same standards as you do. Only when you know the parents will you know what your child might be exposed to when they visit their house. A good rule of thumb: If you can't be friends with the parents your grandkids can't be friends with their kids.

How many times have we blamed kids gone bad for getting in the wrong crowd, but where were the parents when that happened? Many good parents are just too busy and it sneaks up on them. What erases the borders in a child's mind so they are open to hanging out with other kids who were experimenting with sex and drugs?

We must teach our grandchildren how to spot trouble when we're not there and to say no. Kids will argue with you when other parents have other rules, but you must hold your ground and teach your children to do the same.

Rebecca Hagelin states in her book, *30 Ways in 30 Days to Save Your Family,* "Teach them (your kids) the character qualities they should be seeking in their friends – loyalty, kindness, respect toward their parents and others in authority and honesty, to name a few."[5]

# MEDIA INFLUENCE

In this day of media onslaught children spend over five hours per day with electronic media while only having minutes of conversation with their parents.[6]

The amount of garbage our grandchildren are exposed to is unbelievable. The foul language, sexual references, bad attitudes, disrespect, let alone the barrage of information about what identifies one as cool, is enormous. If kids don't have the right clothing, the right shoes, or the right super hero on their backpack, they think they are less important than kids who do, and those kids will let them know it, too!

AWESOME GRANDPARENTING PRINCIPLE: MEDIA'S GOAL IS TO CONTROL YOUR GRANDCHILD'S FUTURE AND FINANCES. AWESOME GRANDPARENTS CONTROL ALL OF THE MEDIA ALL OF THE TIME

In our home Debbie and I do not have cable or even television. Anything we want Anthony to see we intentionally buy on DVD. He has his own player, but we totally control what he sees and how much time he spends on it. He gets a mix of secular, like PAW Patrol, and Bible teaching, like Superbook. PAW Patrol is one of the best shows on television for kids. It actually teaches something; caring for others, teamwork, good attitude, and community service.

You must know what your grandchildren are hearing and seeing at all times! You are in a war for your grandchild's heart and mind. Determine that you will win. Control all of the media all the time.

# THERE IS HOPE!

No matter what condition your grandchildren are in now, there is hope! God can intervene. Prayer works. But, while praying and asking God for help, we, as parents and grandparents, must be willing to rightly assess the problem and apply radical intervention now! Their salvation starts with us, their parents and grandparents.

You must be willing to apply pressure, for you may be God's greatest tool. When you pray for them, pray harder for yourself. Right praying releases the strength to do what is right, whether that means interfering with the status quo, or getting out of the way, and keeping your hands off, so God can have His way.

Perhaps you are faced with transitioning your retirement priorities for your grandchildren. Know this; the life you lose is for the lives you save. Give your life and it will come back to you, pressed, down, shaken together, and running over.[7] I know. Been there. Done that. Got the T-Shirt and a new life full of joy and laughter. You'll get back far more than you give!

# The Rest of the Story

We are guardians of our grandson Anthony and we take that very serious. God has allowed us to be a conduit to pour good things in his life; respect, accountability, manners, and a knowledge of Jesus. We get Anthony and Bella together every weekend. We have them spend as much time as they can with their mother. Bella says, "I miss my daddy in heaven." What a blessing to care for these small children.

> *"But now the LORD my God has given me rest on every side,*
> *so that there is neither adversary nor evil confronting me."*
>
> 1 KINGS 5:4 (AMP)

## ENDNOTES

1. From American Cancer Society, from article entitled: *Health Risks of Second Hand Smoke.* Included is: second hand smoke is known to cause cancer. It has more than seven thousand chemicals, including at least seventy that can cause cancer.
2. Exodus 20:6 NIV, "But showing love to a thousand generations of those who love me and keep my commandments."
3. Couch surfers, what the young people in our church called themselves. They live on someone's couch and when their welcome is worn out they move to somebody else's house and couch, with a story that would tear your heart out and open your wallet.
4. John Maxwell, *Failing Forward*, available on amazon.com.
5. Rebecca Hagelin, *30 Ways in 30 Days to Save Your Family.* Washington DC, Regnery Publishing, 2009. p. 72.
6. *Applied Developmental Phycology 23,* National Institute on Media and the Family, 2002, pages 157 to 178. A normative study of family media habits, by Douglas Gentile and David A. Walsh.
7. Luke 6:38.

## Debbie's To Do List ———→

- ☑ Sweep the House
- ☑ Have Anthony Check the Mouse Traps by the Furnace
- ☑ Make Sam and Anthony Stop Jumping on the Bed
- ☑ Read the Word
- ☑ Go Check on Mom and See How She's Doing with the Great-Grandkids
- ☑ Visit Grandson at the Jail

# Chapter Nine

## The Religion Factor

*···❦···*

## SAM

*Research* shows that people who have a strong, active faith, who pray and read the Bible, generally do better in life across the board. They are healthier, live longer, cope better, recover quicker and have better social lives and marriages.[1]

## NOT A RELIGION

Christianity is different than all other religions. All world religions have their values and principles, and most have their conditions for getting into Heaven. They are all works based, in order to get whatever they promise in the afterlife.

Christianity is different. It is relationship based. It is the only religion that claims its founder, Jesus Christ, is still alive. It is the only one that says God will forgive you if you simply trust your life into His hands, accept that you are sinful, that means fallen way short of God's holiness, and accept the fact that Jesus, God himself, died for you. You simply admit your brokenness, and humbly accept His forgiveness.

*Come to me all you that labor and are heavy-laden*
*and overburdened and I will cause you to rest.*
MATTHEW 11:28 (NIV)

Christianity is not a religion of works. It is a religion of rest. It says there is absolutely nothing you can do to earn God's approval and that you must accept that and stop trying. It says what you do is rest in the work that God himself, Jesus, does on your behalf.

When your life falls apart you do two things: 1) trust Jesus, and 2) rest. Your rest is the indicator dial on the dashboard of your faith that indicates if you are indeed trusting. Is your meter weighing in on the low side? Give your heart to Jesus. No matter what has happened, no matter where you are, you can start fresh today, and make a difference for your children and grandchildren tomorrow. Here's a simple prayer you can model your own after:

*Jesus, I admit that I am a sinner and I need you. I give my heart, my*
*mind, and my whole life to you. I accept you as my personal Savior.*
*Come into my life. I accept you and your Holy Spirit. Teach me your*
*ways. Draw me close to you. Open up your Word to me and I will seek*
*out good people of faith who can help me grow in my faith and I will*
*follow you all the days of my life.*

If you just accepted Jesus as your savior go to the contact information at the back of this book and let us know. We'd like to put some free literature in your hands, pray for you and answer any questions you might have.

# HOME CHURCH

Debbie and I have been a part of traditional, and not so traditional churches all our lives. We have never forsaken fellowship with the saints, no matter how rude some have been at times. We forgive them, because He forgave us. However, after nearly sixty years in traditional western culture church we decided we needed a change. We just could not get some of our kids and our grandkids to go to church. So, we decided to become a church. According to the book of Ephesians in the Bible, chapter five, verse four through fifteen, a husband and wife, meeting together with the Spirit of God, is a church. The Bibles' original word for church is ekklesia,[2] which simply means those who are called out of the world. We are that. We wanted to reach our children and grandchildren, so we started having church in the front room of our house.

## SO MANY WOUNDED AND LOST YOUNG PEOPLE

We had church for about two years with average attendance of four to eight people. During that time, according to our records, we had more than a hundred young people pass through our front room. Our grandkids, then teenagers, brought their friends with them. We'd get a nice group built up and then the next Sunday we'd have no one because part or even all our congregation got thrown in jail that week! We had prostitutes, druggies, couch surfers and addicts of all kinds come into our living room and tell their stories.

Many did not feel accepted by the institutional church, but they were hungry for God. We scratched our heads as we tried to learn to minister to all their crazy needs. Some didn't have a home to go back to after service, so we'd always have a meal after our meetings. It was probably the only decent meal a lot of them got all week.

The best thing that happened to us was that we changed our definition of church. We dismissed the idea that the church was a holy place, in a holy building, led by a holy man, at certain holy times of the week. Our marriage and our house became the church. One day a young man walked through our kitchen and said, "You guys are the real deal, and this is a real church." Our marriage was the only decent example of a marriage a lot of them ever saw.

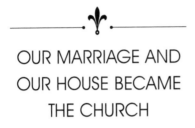

## OUR MARRIAGE AND OUR HOUSE BECAME THE CHURCH

Sometimes we would just have a bunch of little kids so we'd dance to worship music in the kitchen, have what I would call a whacked out Bible story, play the guitar and sing songs in the family room, and have a craft time at the kitchen table and then a snack. They thought having church and faith in the home was the way it was supposed to be. They didn't know any different.

# THE PRAYER CIRCLE

With the kids we would take turns putting each of us in the middle of a prayer circle and we would lay hands on each other and pray. They loved it. They loved the attention and the positive words said over them.

One day I said in the adult group meeting that I felt a certain young man needed encouragement, that we should all gather around him and lay hands on him and pray. So we the adults gathered and prayed and when I opened my eyes, evidently the children, who were playing in the other room had heard me. They were right there in the group with their hands on his knees, praying right along with us. No one told them they couldn't do that, they were used to doing it, so they just did.

One day we were in the middle of songs and our seven-year old grandson said Jesus gave him a vision and he had to stop and draw it.

It was an awesome picture of Jesus with his hands around the neck of a snake, putting it in a cage.

One time Bella, who is Zachary's little girl, and Anthony's sister, went off to the bathroom. When she came back she said, "I saw my daddy and Jesus." We said, "Oh really. What were they doing?" She said, "They were holding hands and dancing."

## EXPLAINING DEATH TO A CHILD

The day after Zachary died it fell to my duty to explain to Bella, then five, that their daddy had died. I desperately prayed for wisdom. What do you say to a little child when they will never see their daddy again? I was impressed by the Holy Spirit to go around the house and gather lots of pictures of friends and family and have Bella point to the people, tell me their names and if they were alive or if they had died and gone to heaven. I pointed to her daddy's picture and asked where he was and then gently explained what had happened. At first she said no, her daddy was back at her house. I replied, "No, he is in heaven" and I explained the accident and for the first two or three times she said, "No. He's not dead." Slowly she understood. I just spent a lot of time with her in my arms and explained how God had provided moms and dads and grandmas and granddads for when a mom or dad goes to heaven.

Several months later she said she saw her daddy in a dream. We asked her if he said anything and she simply said, "Yes." So we asked, "What did he say?" and she said, "He said, ""Accept."" Interesting, coming from a six-year old.

She and Anthony have adjusted well. Debbie recently said something profound. She said Anthony and Bella will have to experience new kinds of healing as they grow up and come into new seasons in their lives. I am so glad we will be here for them and have this awesome faith in Jesus to give us wisdom and strength for the journey.

# TRUE SPIRITUALITY

Watching parents model a spiritual life with each other is powerful. Including the whole family is essential. You can't just tell them about God, you have to humbly nurture a vital, living relationship with God for yourself, in front of your children. Its show and tell time. If you tell it, but don't show it they will reject it.

Don't drop your kids off at church. You go to church for you and take them with you, and choose a good, vital church, with lots of Word teaching, faith and prayer. Your kids will know the difference between your telling and your showing.

READ THE BIBLE IN FRONT OF YOUR CHILDREN AND KNOW IT WELL ENOUGH TO ANSWER THEIR QUESTIONS

Sit down at the kitchen table with your spouse, read the Bible and pray together. Make it a place any subject can be talked about, without fear of reprisal or ridicule. Anything from sex, to money, the kids, and work, anything at all. Nothing is out of bounds for discussion. Pray together about everything. This is real church. This is what you want your kids to see as church. This way they will learn they are to have church in their home. If you're single, do it for you and the kids.

Read the Bible in front of your children and know it well enough to answer their questions.

Reveal problems you're facing, age appropriate, and let them see you pray and watch how God answers along with you.

Fellowship with godly people in your home over meals.

Humbly tell your kids you are sorry when you mess up. Tell them you don't understand when you really don't understand God or life.

Stand in faith through trials. Let them see you struggle where it's appropriate for their age.

Let them see grandpa and grandma waltzing in the kitchen. Cultivate a great love affair with your spouse. Get down on the floor and wrestle with your grandchildren.

## LET THEM SEE GRANDPA AND GRANDMA DANCE IN THE KITCHEN

If you don't have a believing or participating spouse then dance with them yourself. Many a young man has been saved years later because he had a believing, praying grandmother. Consistency and persistency is the name of the game in the war for your grandchildren. You may lose some battles, but if you are persistent over a long period of time you will see results.

Take your kids with you on local missions to love and serve people. I love the fact that my son-in-law Chris takes his kids, Grace and Ethan, to the downtown Seoul, Korea, train station where they hand out bags of food to the homeless. They get to see the other side of life. They learn to love everyone, become less selfish and more serving.

Send them off to a foreign country mission trip so they can see just how good they've got it back here at home. Joel Osteen says, "You can store up blessings and favor by living a life of excellence and integrity that will affect generations to come."[3]

# PROTECTING YOUR CHILDREN

Many in the church prayed for Stacy and Zachary's dad to be healed and when he wasn't they were wounded and they have been cool toward God and the church ever since. Something went wrong in this situation. Years later when their mom was diagnosed with M.S. she recovered, but that did not matter. Her children turned away from God when Tom wasn't healed, but did not turn back to God when Debbie was.

Anger at God, for any excuse, can simply be a reason to slough off the commitment God demands for control of your life. In situations where tender young minds are involved, extra care must be taken to council and nurture for we never know what might happen tomorrow. Debbie and I know how quickly someone can be taken. We must teach our children to pray and to have faith, but we must wisely teach them to cope and recover when things don't go as hoped.

A strong vital relationship with God in the home and in fellowship with God's people makes a huge difference in the life of your young person.

## ⊹——— *The Rest of the Story* ———⊹

Never, ever give up. Never stop having faith. As Lester Sumrall, the founder of LeSea Broadcasting, always said, "Feed your faith and starve your doubts." Do that and you will see the salvation of God for your children and grandchildren and all the seeds you sow will sprout up in a thousand generations after you.[4]

*"Be still and rest in the Lord; wait for Him and patiently lean yourself upon Him; fret not yourself because of him who prospers in his way, because of the man who brings wicked devices to pass."*
PSALMS 37:7 (AMP)

## ENDNOTES

1. WebMD, feature article: *Spirituality May Help People Live Longer*, copyright 1999.
2. The Greek word *Ekklesia*, pronounced ek-klay-see'-ah, *Strong's Concordance of the Bible*.
3. Joel Osteen, *I Declare: 31 Promises to Speak Over Your Life* (NY, NY, FaithWords, 2012) p. 33.
4. Deuteronomy 7:9 "Because of this, know that Jehovah your God, He is God, the faithful God, keeping the covenant and mercy to those who love Him, and to those who keep His commands, to a thousand generations."

## Sam's To Do List ————✦

☑  Pray With Debbie

☑  Mow the Yard

☑  Play with Anthony in the Sand Box

## Chapter Ten

# *A Summer Place*

··· ❧◦❧ ···

## DEBBIE

*Anthony* came to visit on the day his daddy went to Heaven. Zachary's fiancée was severely injured in the accident and has ongoing physical problems. We are greatly saddened by the hurt she must endure every day of her life now. We love her very much and are proud of the hard, but wise decision, she made to give us guardianship of Anthony. We want to make her proud of him. Our goal is to see that he becomes the man God wants him to be.

The first few days were a blur. We were asking major questions while having to plan a funeral. Where do our lives go from here? Which casket do we pick? How will we care for Anthony and hold down two jobs?

# OUR FINAL GOOD-BYE

Zachary's funeral went as well as any funeral could go. My strong base of awesome grandmothers, family and friends all came out to support me. Many tears were shed over the loss of one so young.

When people asked how we were being so positive we found ourselves saying we were making a withdrawal from a bank account of faith we had been investing in for a long time.

Sam and Logan preached the final powerful service and at the close people were invited up to the casket to say their final good-by to Zachary and then file out to their cars for the trip to the grave. However, instead of going past the casket where there was only death and a sad ending, people turned left at the front pew, instinctively going where they knew there was life and a new beginning. It was a testament to our faith and the power of that service.

They filed by us, shaking hands, hugging us and commenting on how significant and meaningful the preaching and our faith had been to them. It was a testimony to God's presence in that service.

We had a big crowd at our house for a meal after the service. Anthony sat on Sam's lap. It was the first evidence of the strong bond they would form in the coming days.

# A NEW BOND IS FORGED

Due to complications at birth Anthony was born dead. The doctors worked long and hard, and unlike Kit, they managed to revive him. He was in the hospital for the first three weeks of his life. The first week was spent in intensive care. We didn't know if he would survive or, if he did, what brain trauma he might have to live with. Sam and I went to visit him in those first days and he lifted him out of the tiny bed and held him in a rocking chair, praying in the Spirit over him all the while. For several hours they rocked and prayed, rocked and prayed.

For the first year of his life Anthony was on anti-seizure drugs. As a nurse I observed him and saw visible effects of the medication. He was acutely sensitive to any loud noise or fast movement in the room. He would lock on to your eyes and stare right there as you moved. One little laughter or cough and he would start crying or go into hysterics. He would have nothing to do with Sam.

It was interesting to watch the transformation as within just a few hours of arriving at our house Anthony began to cling to Sam and now they are as tight as any father and son could be, perhaps even more so.

## SAM ADJUSTS

Sam was devastated at Zachary's death and perplexed at Anthony's arrival. He had plans! He had been sure in his mind of what God wanted to do in his life in this season. He and I had spent many hours around the kitchen table talking, praying, planning, envisioning the next season as we downsized the Granpa Cratchet business in order to devote ourselves to publishing several books Sam had written over the years. He wasn't sure about taking on an eighteen-month old, but Anthony soon worked his way into Sam's heart and now he wouldn't have it any other way.

# SAM
## THE WRITING BEGINS

Right after our marriage Debbie saw the long hard hours I was working in the business and the deep frustration and depression I was experiencing. She bought me a journal and told me to write, something her counselor had told her to do when Tom was getting sick.

I remember my early entries went something like this; God, your Word is dry and the heavens are like brass and I have work to do, see you tomorrow. But Debbie kept encouraging me and I kept writing. Over the months I began to loosen up and my pen began to flow. She and I would open to a passage of scripture and insights would pour onto the pages of my journal, which had now been switched to a computer in order to keep up with the pace.

Out of those insights a book would emerge, and another, and then another. That writing, that flowing, taught me how to hear God's voice. It has been my salvation and it has become my great joy in life. If you get nothing else from this book I urge you to get a journal and begin writing. The point is not to write, but to open your heart and journal all your doubts, fears, questions, insights and impressions as the Spirit of God begins to emerge. The trickle will become a stream in the desert and the stream will become a river of refreshing. If the melody of your heart has gone silent, then write! In the writing your heart will find the tune again, and learn to sing.

God oftentimes throws us a curve ball and while we're balling our eyes out He's asking, "Will you trust me?" Most of the time when we want stuff, even when we want to do something great for Him, all He wants from us is our trust. He'd rather have our trust than anything we can produce. You can tell Him you love Him all you want, but until you trust Him the words are hollow.

> IF THE TUNE OF YOUR HEART HAS GONE SILENT, THEN WRITE! IN THE WRITING YOUR HEART WILL FIND THE TUNE AGAIN, AND LEARN TO SING.

## DEBBIE TAKES A LEAVE

Debbie took six weeks leave from work to care for Anthony so I could get ready for the summer Granpa Cratchet tour. It soon became evident she could not go back to work and adequately care for Anthony, So, after thirty-nine years of service in a rewarding career as a nurse in the intensive care unit, she retired. She let go of what had been her identity.

There were a lot of endings in those days, most of the time without knowing just what the new beginning would be. But that's the way of trust. You must simply believe that God knows what he is doing and step into the unknown, fully trusting that God is able to make it all turn out right, to make a new beginning where none can be seen. Easy to say, hard to do.

Unsure of himself and out of his usual surroundings, this little eighteen-month old boy did not want us to be out of sight. He drug his toys to whatever room we were in and we set up a little bed at the end of our master bedroom for him to sleep in. Those first nights he would go to sleep between us or on the foot of our bed and then we'd move him down to his bed. The moments when I carried him in my arms, asleep, totally innocent, totally at the mercy of life and what it might hand him, he began to work his way into my heart.

They were hard months of adjustment for Debbie and me. Daily schedule, personal relationship, romance, finances, and time in the Word were all challenged by this new little guy in our family.

Then, of all things to do, Debbie went and got a dog, while I was out of town I might add. I came home to find this little cotton ball on four legs running around and falling all over itself. Just great, I thought. Just what we need. Right in the middle of all this nice, comfortable, predictable life gone to more chaos than a tornado in a mobile home park, why don't we throw in a dog! At first the dog was like Anthony used to be, she didn't want anything to do with me. Then one day I cornered her and scratched her just in the right spot on her rump, she leaned into it and we have been best friends ever since

# *The Rest of the Story*

We had a house full of kids that summer when Grace and Ethan, our daughter Kimberly's kids, came to be with us from Korea. Debbie and Anthony joined them touring with me, doing Granpa Cratchet shows at fairs. That summer I fell in love with Anthony as he followed me around in his baggy shorts and crooked hat. I had lost one son, and now I had gained a son.

The song I titled this chapter after says it all about that summer of '14:

*There's a summer place*
*Where it may rain or storm*
*Yet I'm safe and warm*
*For within that summer place*
*Your Arms [Jesus and Anthony] reach out to me*
*And my heart is free*
*From all care, for it knows*
*There are no gloomy skies*
*When seen through the eyes*
*Of those who are blessed with love*
*And the sweet secret of A summer place*
*Is that it's anywhere, when two people share*
*All their hopes, all their dreams, and all their love*[1]

*"Return unto thy rest, O my soul; for the*
*LORD hath dealt bountifully with thee."*
PSALMS 116:7 (KJV)

# ENDNOTES

*1. A Summer Place,* written by Mack Discant and Max Steiner, published by Lyrics@Warner/Chappell Music, Inc. debuted in the 1959 film by the same title, staring Sandra Dee and Troy Donahue. Many recorded the popular song even though it was not the theme of the movie. Percy faith and his orchestra made it a number one hit for nine weeks in 1960. It became a period piece and was featured in more than twenty films and television shows.

## Sam & Debbie's To Do List ⟶⟶

- ☑ Slow Dance in the Kitchen
- ☑ Tuck Anthony in for the Night after an NCIS rerun
- ☑ Make Room for a New Baby
- ☑ Sam/Debbie/Anthony Dance in the Living Room to Lou Christy Oldies

# Chapter Eleven

# Falling Off the Bicycle

··· ⊰⊱ ···

## SAM

*You* know the old saying you always use when it's time to do something you haven't done for a while, "It's like riding a bicycle." That's supposed to mean, if you haven't done it in a while it will come back to you. Once you know, you always know. Raising kids; like riding a bicycle, right? Not. It's a whole new world out there baby! Things have changed since us baby boomers were growing up in the nineteen fifties. And, things have changed in society since we were raising our kids in the nineteen seventies.

What does this mean? It means that, while some principles are universal and remain pillars we can depend upon, how we apply those might need to be adjusted. It's a whole new ball game out there in terms of:

- What our kids are being taught
- The kind of peer pressure our kids are experiencing

- What they are exposed to at schools
- What they are no longer being taught at school
- What they are exposed to in media
- The amount of time kids now have with media
- What they are exposed to when they visit other family's homes

Rebecca Hagelin states in her book "We've got to teach our children sound values at home so that when they are confronted with damaging messages outside the home, they can recognize them as such and know when to reject them."[1] We must understand what this war means in terms of how we will protect, and be proactive, in raising our grandchildren and great-grandchildren. If you are not outright responsible for your grandchildren, you still play a significant role in their future. As we grandparents get back on the bicycle of raising children we must not assume that what we did fifty or sixty years ago will work today. If we are going to get back on the bicycle we must ride it well! We cannot afford to make our grandchildren an experiment. We have to get it right the first time, this time. We can't just send them off to the public school and expect them to be raised with a worldview consistent with the one we hold as Christians. We must get a clear vision of who our enemy is and create a battle plan to save our children. Which brings us to our first bicycle principle.

# BICYCLE PRINCIPLES
## HAVE A VISION FOR YOUR GRANDCHILD

 Know where the bicycle is going at all times. To be effective in this brave, new world you must have a clear, written vision of what you want your grandchildren to be when they are adults. If you can't clearly state it on paper you will not be able to write it on their minds and hearts. Writing it out and looking at it regularly helps you remember where the battle

lines are and evaluate how you are doing in the war. We want Anthony to:

- Know and trust Jesus as his personal savior
- Be a blessing to others
- Become a responsible member of society
- Be productive
- Be respectful
- Have good manners
- Stay out of drugs
- Learn to read and write in at least the seventy-five percentile
- Have math and comprehension skills that can compete in the world
- Be able to critically think with inductive and deductive reasoning
- Be able to make great decisions and stand on his own two feet
- Have a Biblical world view
- Know how to handle money
- Have the skills necessary to choose a good mate and have a healthy productive family of his own
- Achieve an education on the level he needs to succeed in the vocation that is best for him

## DON'T LET SOMEONE ELSE STEER YOUR BIKE

Be proactive and involved in every area of your grandchild's life and start early. At three years old we are teaching Anthony to work and earn money for  what he wants. We're not going to wait for school to teach him that five years from now. This means you must proactively monitor everything:

TV, internet, music, reading materials, anything that exposes his mind to anything. Keep the chain oiled!

## MONITOR MEDIA

This means not just closely monitoring what Anthony watches on TV (we don't have internet, cable or open air TV in our home). What we want him to see, we buy on DVD. That way he is not automatically learning that whatever he decides to watch is ok and that everything on the TV is just fine. He gets to choose from the DVDs we have and he sees us watching and thinking in the store and consciously choosing what is right and wrong. He watches us to learn how to do it himself.

## IT'S SHOW AND TELL TIME

In the war you cannot tell your grandchild the way it should be, and then live in a way inconsistent with your words. They will reject your word and also learn  that your word is not trustworthy. You have to consistently model the behavior you want in front of them. If you want them to have a good marriage then you must model a good marriage in front of them. If you want them to be good communicators then you must model good communication all the time! To build their life you must monitor yours. If you want them to handle money right, then you must handle money right and have them involved in the money management in your home. You can't just tell them, you have to show them. If you don't show it, they will never know it. Adjust your seat to the right height.

## START EARLY

Public schools are exposing our toddlers to things we didn't get until we were adults, and now this includes things we wouldn't want to know about at all as adults. Starting early to teach your child anything is what it takes to win this war. We began to teach Anthony money management as soon as he came into our home at age two. We found he loved to run the vacuum cleaner, so we let him run it, even though he ran into things, knocked things over, and dinged things. We let him do it and lavishly praised him and, gave him a bank and a quarter. At age three he knows we buy him what he needs and he has to buy what he wants.

So he works and counts his money, even though he is usually way off. We carefully time his purchase to teach patience without discouragement. We encourage him to work, earn and achieve what he wants, and never discourage him from the process. We don't care that he may want a toy that's fifteen dollars and he only has eight. We let him hand the money to the clerk. He has learned that work is fun and has already strongly attached the idea that work gets you what you want. If he can learn the English language at eighteen months he can learn lots of other things too. We watch whatever he is interested in and use that to tell him and show him life principles.

## LAVISH WITH LOVE

There is a great book called *The Five Love Languages*[2] by Dr. Gary Chapman. Get this book and determine that you will expose your young grandchild to all the  languages. We can't just show them love by buying them things, although gifting is one of the ways we can show love. We lavish Anthony with lots of hugs and kisses. He is just now developing his love language so now is the time to show him all the languages and help him be comfortable with all of them. He's going to have to deal with all kinds of people to succeed, knowing all the universal love languages will help him be able to meet, greet, connect and communicate with all kinds of people. This will be extremely valuable in life. Make sure those tires are properly inflated.

## DISCIPLINE

 Toddlers think they are masters of the world around them, but they must learn obedience. Time outs as necessary, and Anthony has had a few of these. And, we are not afraid of spanking, applied sparsely and with wisdom.

If the Garden of Eden taught us anything, if the world around us is showing us anything, it is that love without boundaries is disastrous. We let Anthony do things with us that our parents would have never done. We let him help us cook, clean, drive the tractor, mow the yard, and hammer a nail.

Everything we do we let him do with us, very closely monitored for safety and for learning. In this way we are teaching him to explore, to be adventurous, open to life, and that learning is fun. At the same time we are teaching him to think and to have boundaries, as we explain why the boundaries are there. We keep it simple, but we let him do things. We are learning patience because he really slows down the process. But, slower might be good for us too, and it's definitely good for him to be involved. Don't forget to oil the gears.

# STRUCTURE

Of course, you understand how much they are depending upon you. I look at Anthony and see how innocent and incapable he is of surviving life. He  would not survive without us. But, it's much more. Knowing they can depend on you, having consistent structures with meals, playtime and bedtime is necessary for mental and emotional health.

Debbie and I have a tandem bike and we pull Anthony behind in a Peapod.

# ✦ ————— *The Rest of the Story* ————— ✦

Rest assured, awesome grandparents can get "back on the bike" and ride it better than ever. You may need some adjustment time. You may be a little wobbly at first, but you can do it.

*". . . ask where the good way is, and walk in it, and you will find rest for your souls."*

JEREMIAH 6:16B (NIV)

## ENDNOTES

1. Rebecca Hagelin, *30 Ways in 30 Days to Save Your Family* (Washington, DC, Regnery Publishing Inc, 2009), p.13.
2. Dr. Gary Chapman, *The Five Love Languages,* (Northfield Publishers, Moody, Chicago, Illinois, 1995) Available on amazon.com.

## Debbie's To Do List ————➤

- ☑ Buy Some Training Wheels
- ☑ Call Malachi for Play Time
- ☑ Shut Off the TV
- ☑ Buy Anthony a Bike to Ride with Me

# Chapter Twelve

# Getting Back on the Bicycle

···❦·❦···

## SAM

*Over* the past two years Anthony has seen excellent physical and personal growth. When he came to live with us he was eighteen months old, now he's three and a half at this time. People who have known him from the beginning often comment on his positive progress, while it has been challenging for us at times.

Anthony spent his first week in the neonatal intensive care unit. It has been determined that neonatal intensive care babies show certain behavior patterns later, such as over effort to control.

At age two testing by child psychology professionals from his birth hospital showed him to be in the normal range for physical and mental capacities, somewhat ahead cognitively and a little behind in speech.

This explained some of the frustration type behavior we saw, as he would understand things, but be unable to express himself in regard to his surroundings or needs. During his first summer with us our grandkids, Grace and Ethan, taught him sign language and that seemed to bring a measure of relief from anxiety attacks.

He also has exhibited the nicu-baby tendency to exert an overdrive effort to control his environment. At times he would become emotionally overwhelmed and present extreme crying episodes. However, he has become very close to me (Sam), we are best buddies now, and the episodes seem to be cycling further apart.

We have used a wide range of responses to help Anthony cope. We use mechanisms such as:

1. **Redirection:** showing him something else that is fun besides what is frustrating him

2. **Sensory stimulation:** keeping things going at a pace that doesn't allow him time to get fixated on a frustrating problem

3. **Wide public adult level exposure:** keeping him meeting new people, showing him that it is safe to see and be seen is helping him grow in social skills

4. **Wide range of playmates:** keeps him stimulated and growing in relational skills with kids his own age

5. **New Toys:** a constant, but well timed, flow of new toys keeps him growing in skills and cognitive reasoning. A new toy introduces a new part of the world, through which we can teach him skills and about how the world works, while we stimulate sensory awareness

6. **A consistent punishment system:** this way there are no surprises or a sense of unsureness as a side effect

7. **A wide range of reward:** this keeps him in a state of expectancy about his future

8. **Maintaining family connections:** keeps a sense of family and identity

9. **Maintaining ample time with mommy, his sister and other grandmother:** this has done a lot to help him retain a sense of regularity and structure

10. **Travel:** we took him on a plane trip to Washington D.C. to see our son Cameron and visit friends. This provided a lot of stimulation and information, which keeps his world turning and growing

11. **Reading books:** Provides a window to the world, fosters growth in understanding, in relationships, and in skills we want him to develop. He loves tractors and machinery of any and all kinds. Then when we travel, whether close or far we look for what we have seen in the books

12. **Media control:** even at this young age we are very careful about what he watches and keep all exposure age appropriate. We don't have cable or open air TV. We only buy DVDs of what we want him exposed to and then give him lots of room to choose

So much could be said about the things we have to do to foster mental, spiritual and emotional growth. The most valuable thing is to pay close attention to your grandchild's specific and unique needs and discover creative, organic ways to stimulate and teach with as much hands on for the child and as much personal involvement as you can.

Even though we are old hats at this we have fallen off the child rearing bicycle a time or two this year. We never assume we understand or know enough. We are always reading new books and asking parents and grandparents lots of questions about their kids, querying about how they handle their children, and probing the many aspects of child rearing. We never, ever assume we know all there is to know. If we want Anthony to grow we must stay a step ahead of him, and that means we need to be growing.

Here are a few more refresher bicycle tips that might help you stave off a scrape or two.

# BICYCLE PRINCIPLES
## PROVIDE ABUNDANT SOCIAL TIME

Even though you may be sixty-five, if you are raising a child you can connect with middle aged and young mothers for play dates, and outings to places like the park or the zoo. Grandparents often have access to things parents don't because we have more resources. We have a museum membership.

## MAINTAIN STRONG FAMILY TIES

In today's world children are often divided between grandparent's homes. It's so important to maintain a strong and consistent sense of family. Anthony spends  time with his sister Bella every weekend. We work hard at connecting Anthony with his mom, his other grandmother, my dad, Debbie's parents, and all the cousins, too. It provides a sense of belonging and identity. By keeping family in the center he is learning this value; that family is central and a high value. Ok, time to take off the training wheels.

## BUILD A STRONG SPIRITUAL LIFE

Since we had home church for a couple of years the kids have experienced the strong impact of having "home church." We had (Still do) bible stories in the bedroom, dance to bible songs in the kitchen, share prayer requests, do Bible centered crafts, and lay hands on each other and pray blessings over each other. Anything that's done in church we do in the home. Home is church! We have found that young ones can be far more sensitive to spiritual things than we give them credit for. Let them know God loves them with words and hugs. Anthony says his daddy is in heaven, so we ask God to bless his daddy in heaven just like we pray for family members on earth.

Don't just take your children to church, go with them. You can't just tell them, you have to participate and show them. Connecting with a great church teaches your grandchildren the value of connecting with other Christians, being in Christian fellowship, under teaching and authority.

## TEACH MANNERS

Please and thank you, inside voices, and "May I be excused from the table" will have an impact on the rest of their lives. Everything we know we learned in  kindergarten right? Teaching manners is teaching respect and inserting value into our daily actions. Learning simple manners opens the door to learning complex social issues later. Learning manners teaches the golden rule. Keep that bike out of the side ditch!

## PROVIDE GOOD HEALTH AND NUTRITION

You have to start reading labels! Keep the sugar at a minimum. Diet and exercise effect kids just like it does grandparents. Kids are known for being picky eaters. I have heard many stories about kids sitting at the table until they eat that "green thing". Be creative and moderate with your food choices. Teach them to eat what you set before them, but also know their interests and be creative with those vitamins. Doctor visits are needed and immunizations as you believe. We spaced Anthony's out a lot to assure his little body could handle the cocktail of chemicals doctors recommend. We have a great doctor and we trust him. Know your doctor! Know your bike mechanic, too.

## LEARN THE ART OF NEGOTIATING

We do a lot of negotiating with Anthony, a lot more than our parents would have ever done with us, but we like it. It teaches him to think and to communicate with us. It teaches him to reason things out, to think through what he really wants and to make partnerships. Until further notice, use anything and everything you can to teach your child valuable lessons. We often laugh at, and love, the way Anthony will negotiate with us for five more minutes of his favorite activities. If he will talk to us and reason with us now, we'll have a lot better chance of this being the pattern when he is a teenager and away from our protection and control. Our goal is to build a functioning, thinking, mature adult, who will stay connected with us. Think about where you want your bike to go and plan a route.

## LOTS OF POSITIVE EXPOSURE

As grandparents we have a much better perspective to all that's going on around us. Hopefully we're not as wrapped up in careers and climbing the ladder at this later time in life. As such we have a great opportunity to expose our grandkids to the exciting world around them. Take them to the zoo, museums, the library, have them ride on the neighbor's combine. (Anthony loves tractors and diggers.) We wonder together at everything, birds nests, sunsets, the moon and stars, flowers and nature. As grandparents we have the time to do things with and for them that our parents were just too busy for. Slow your bike down and enjoy the scenery. It's not just about arriving, it's also about the journey.

## PAY ATTENTION!

Anthony loves to have us watch while he does things. Paying lots of attention to the things that matter to them instills value into them. Read to them, play with  them, or just watch them jump. I am very good at getting down on the floor and playing with our grandkids. As my character Granpa Cratchet says, "Everyone should be five years old at least once a day."

## BE ACTIVELY INVOLVED IN THEIR EDUCATION

 You can no longer automatically expect the public school to raise your child in a way consistent with your Christian worldview or Godly moral values. You must be involved in every aspect of their education. Whether private or public, never automatically assume any school will give your grandchild a better education than another. Check it out! You have to monitor every aspect of their education and be proactive in asking for, even demanding, a quality education for your grandchild. Read the curriculum, talk with teachers, interview the principal, and get to know your superintendent of schools. Find out if they are going to kowtow to every federal mandate and compromise your child's moral education and spiritual foundation to acquire federal funds. What the superintendent is, flows down to the classroom and effects your grandchild.

Check out home schooling and find out if that is right for you. Home schooling has really developed and home schooled children many times outperform other school structures. There is the national association of home schoolers and there will be a home school association in your state. Giving your grandchild a great education begins when you give yourself a great education. And, don't forget to keep your bike tires aired up.

## OUR LAST BICYCLE PRINCIPLE - GIVE YOURSELF AN EDUCATION

We could write a whole book on bicycle riding. So we want to finish by saying this, in all aspects of (grand) child rearing never assume what you know is enough.
Read. A lot. Talk with people, with parents, experts and see what is going on. Always be researching, looking, thinking, talking and acting. You can never know enough and do enough to assure your grandchild will have a great life.

We recommend you read everything you can by Rebecca Hagelin. You will get an eye opener as to what is really going on in our schools, in the media and in our society. Be proactive in every aspect of your grandchild's life. Have standards and don't give up the fight. We are in a war. Be determined to win, and not deterred from your vision for your grandchild's life, even if they are forty.

We are grandparents. We are formidable. We are awesome. We will win the war for our grandchildren!

## ✦——— *The Rest of the Story* ———✦

Every five-year period in your grandchild's growth will present new challenges and require new techniques to solve new challenges, and some of the old ones that carry over. The best thing you can do is rest in knowing that you are making every effort to learn and grow, and that you are also taking care of yourself. Time away in prayer, meditation, in Christian fellowship, and regular getaways with your spouse are all part of taking it all in stride and in a healthy pace.

*"One hand full of rest and patience is better than two fists*
*full of labor and chasing after the wind."*
ECCLESIASTES 4:6 (AMP)

## *Debbie's Bicycle To Do List* —✄

☑   Read a Book on Raising Kids

☑   Have Coffee and Laughs with a Friend

☑   Plan a Night Out with Sam

☑   Go on a Bike Ride with Sam and Anthony

# Chapter Thirteen

# *Connections*

...⚜...

## DEBBIE

*Plugging* into family and friends in the time of crisis is like plugging in an appliance, it connects you to a current that makes things work. It is a flow of sustenance that helps you get out of bed every day. Even if you don't feel like getting your toenails painted, you still have to get out of bed and put one foot in front of the other. If the appliance isn't plugged in its just not going to do what it needs to do. If you will stay connected the flow of fellowship will pour in the power you need to keep on going.

Friends don't always know what to say and sometimes they say the wrong thing, but you overlook that. You just let them express themselves. Sometimes you can even find yourself encouraging them. Just like AC current, courage to keep up the journey flows both directions. Conversation is the flow of life when circumstances are draining your life from you. However, life can flow in the silence. Just be there for someone. Allow them to talk, give a hug, or do an act of kindness such as bring dinner.

*"And holding fast to the Head, from Whom the entire body, supplied and knit together by means of its joints and ligaments, grows with a growth that is from God"* (Colossians 2:19 AMP). In times of great stress you might not feel like getting dressed, you might not feel like eating, but just as you must take physical food, you must take of the nourishment that comes from deep connections to others.

I used to sing this little rhyme when I was a child and it came back to me the summer Zachary died:

*Make new friends, But keep the old*
*One is silver, And the other is gold*

So many old friends came out of the woodwork to support me and I had made many new friends who came to cheer me on. We need cheerleaders in a time like this. If you just let people be who they are they will bring a little warmth during the cold season of your heart's pain.

Here's a few ways to make sure you stay plugged in to the power of connections.

## CALL SOMEONE

If you reach out people will feel more comfortable about reaching out to you. Don't feel rejected if people stop calling once the funeral is over. So many came out to support Sam when Kit died, but in the months afterward no one came, no one called, and that led to the killer thought: no one cares. Don't fall prey to the no-one-cares trap. People care, they just don't know if they can call or stop over. If they are a little unsure the safe thing they do is nothing. When you call, you give them permission to connect with you.

## TEXT SOMEONE

One of the hardest things to do in a time of crisis and stress is to find the right words to say. Texting or emailing is fantastic because it's a great exercise in crafting words. You can do it at your own pace, in your own time and in your own words. It doesn't matter if you have to stop and shed a tear, texting lets you do that in private, and go right back to saying words. You know you have to put one foot in front of the other, sometimes you can get through your day by putting one word in front of the other. The more you say to others, the more they will open up to you.

There are so many, many things you can do to reach out and create a new river of love which will water and bring new life to a barren landscape.

## TAKE A WALK WITH SOMEONE

You know how important exercise is, so go do it with a friend. Walking is great because your emotions will become whatever you put in front of your eyes. If you put green grass, blue skies, red flowers and laughing people in front of your eyes, they will bring you a refreshing moment in the midst of the pain. It's alright to grieve, but you also need to give yourself a moment to forget and laugh. Plus, when you exercise you release chemicals called endorphins. They interact with the receptors in your brain that reduce your perception of pain. Endorphins also trigger positive feelings in the body[1]. I like to think of them as a race of little people from Lord of the Rings. They get into your blood, run around and jump up and down and their energy becomes yours.

## TEA AT THREE

Coffee or tea with a friend is so great because when you go to the coffee shop there's lots of noise and noise means life. Plus, coffee stimulates and so does the conversation. Coffee is a great way to just let people talk.

After Kit died Sam would be out places and just start to bawl. After a while people got used to it. They would just keep on talking while he had a good cry and then he would rejoin them and the conversation would go right on. Don't be afraid to cry in public or it will be really hard to get back out there and stay connected. If you go out you never can tell when you might see something that will set you off, so carry six boxes of tissues with you and people will laugh.

## LOVE THE LITTLE THINGS

If it's hard to love what you're going through, then find little things you can love in the middle of the stress. Read the Word, especially the book of Psalms. Find a great positive book of poetry. Read a great fiction book. Sam loves Seize the Night and Life Expectancy by Dean Koontz. Read some venue you've never read before; history, biography, romance (there are some great Christian romances out there). Check out Mark of the Lion trilogy by Francine Rivers. These were the most impactful books I have ever read outside of the Bible. If you love mystery, yet want a Biblical worldview, read Randy Alcorn's trilogy of books: Dominion, Deadline and Deception.

Plant flowers, or build a model. You get the idea. Bring out an old love you haven't paid attention to in a while. Fill the emptiness with what you love and you put love into the midst of your challenge.

## WRITE IN YOUR JOURNAL

When you write something it gives your mind permission to let go. People do what Sam calls "Court rooming." That is, if they have been through a time of stress involving conflict in relationships, they will find themselves in a mental courtroom, rehashing all the reasons why something shouldn't have happened to them, or why their position was the right one. It's mental obsessing over details and events. It's a natural thing to do. To break the cycle write it down and in the process commit it to God and in the writing let it go. Then, if your mind goes back to it, tell your mind it doesn't have to go over all that again, it's all written down. You can choose your thoughts. Take charge! Write it down and let it go. You can write your way to a new life, to a new you.

## CREATE LITTLE DISTRACTIONS ON PURPOSE

Take a mini five-minute vacation, five times a day, for five days in a row, on purpose. Sit down and make a list of all the things you love to do. Work with your hands. Build something in the woodshop, create a basket of hanging silk flowers, take pictures, whatever it is you love to do, go back to that, and do it again. When Anthony starts to go down the path of an emotional outburst one of the tools I use is distractions. I just change the subject, get real excited about something and his mind and emotions will often go with me to the new place. You can do it to. Distract your mind and your emotions will go to the new place.

Caroline Leaf says in her book, Who Switched Off My Brain, that we can create new thoughts and lay them over the old thoughts and thereby make the old thoughts weaker and fade, as the new thoughts get stronger.[2] You can think yourself to a new life, to a new you.

## EXERCISE & DIET

Sam says he walks around the block every morning. Actually, he has this little block of wood he keeps under the bed. He gets out of bed, pulls out the block, walks around it, puts it back under the bed and crawls back under the blankets.

Buy a Fitbit wrist exercise and calorie tracker and fill out the daily Fitbit app to make sure you are eating the right things.

## BE SOCIAL

Be wise about social media. Whatever you put out there cannot be brought back, but it is a great way to connect with others. It's simple to start, they have made it easy. If you're not sure, find someone to show you the ropes. Learning to use Facebook is a great way to connect and create conversation.

## REACH OUT AND HELP SOMEONE

Do whatever you need to do to get out of the house, to get out with other people; find a part time job, volunteer, or do something for your church. Go help other people who are hurting. Nursing homes are great places to find people who are worse off than you, who can bring you perspective and a new joy that comes through encouraging others. Take action. Press through the pain.

## DEFEAT DEPRESSION

Depression, by its very nature, will weigh you down, slow you down and cause you to disconnect from family and friends. The way to defeat it is to get moving, in spite of the feelings. You must resist and deny the powerful feelings of depression and just start moving. New emotions follow new actions. Do not believe the lie that there is no answer to your dilemma, no new direction after one door is closed.

Depression is, in fact, one of four emotional alarm systems God has built into humans. The other three are fear, guilt and anger. These signals tell us something is amiss in our relationships with others or ourselves. Depression, like all emotional alarm systems, can create such discomfort that it demands our attention. We're forced to acknowledge that a problem exists or the havoc will persist until we confront and resolve it.

Dr. Gary Lovejoy and Dr. Gregory Knopf say in their book, Light on the Fringe; finding hope in the darkness of depression, "Most clients who walk into my (counseling) office live in a world of relational pain. They talk about depression, loneliness, insecurity, never measuring up, resentments and the like. But what they are invariably describing is a frustrated desire to be loved and to love someone in return."[3]

## MAINTAIN AN INNER CORE GROUP

We all have friends or family we are close to. Sometimes it is an effort to maintain these relationships. Remember, one foot in front of the other. The Bible says in Zechariah 4:10 that we should not despise small beginnings.[4] Family can be a powerful ally for you. Lean on them during the difficult times. There may be opportunity in the future for them to lean on you.

*"Praise be to the God and Father of our Lord*
*Jesus Christ, the Father of compassion and the God*
*of all comfort, who comforts us is all our troubles,*
*so that we can comfort those in any trouble with*
*the comfort we ourselves receive from God."*
2 CORINTHIANS 1:3-4 (NIV)

I have shared this comfort with friends and their families in the I.C.U. Having been through illness and death, I have compassion for those who are experiencing it. Sharing comfort multiplies comfort back to you.

I have been leading a circle of girlfriends in a yearly get away for about thirty-five years. We eat together, shop, play games, have a lot of laughs, study the word and pray together and hug each other. What traumas, heartaches and changes we have all been through over that time. It is a time to remember how the Lord carries and sustains us with His mighty power and provision. God's blessing is quite evident in our friendships and how we make time for each other. Laughter is like medicine to the heart and the body.[5] Laugh a lot. Laugh every day. The enemy doesn't know what to do with someone who laughs at trouble.

I can't talk about friends without mentioning my best friend, Sam. My husband has a degree in psychology and I have been his constant client. Seriously, he has been such a strong support. I prayed for a godly man and I definitely got one! We love to do things together; read, hike, travel, spend time with family and friends, or just share a good cup of coffee. Lately, it's been writing this book together. Intentionally cultivate relationship with your spouse. It's worth the investment.

## The Rest of the Story

In the Bible, in the book of Ruth, Naomi had a close relationship with her two daughters-in-law. They had all been through much together.

All three had lost loved ones, mates. In the time of devastation, they had learned to lean on one another, to love one another. Your season of paintless toenails is the time to reach out, to make new friends, or to lean on others. In the leaning you will learn how to help others when it is time for them to lean on you.

You too can find rest, even while you are weeping. Sam knows. God gave him a rest and assurance during the summer after Kit died, even while he was mourning deeply and cried often.

*"May the Lord deal with you as kindly as you have with me. Then Naomi said to her two daughters-in-law. . The LORD grant you that you may find a home and rest, each in the house of her husband! Then she kissed them and they wept aloud."*

RUTH 1:8,9 (AMP)

# ENDNOTES

1. WEBMD.com, article: Exercise and Depression, p. 1.
2. Dr. Caroline Leaf, *Who Switched Off My Brain: Controlling Toxic Thoughts and Emotions*, (Published by Improv Ltd, distributed by Thomas Nelson Publishers, USA, 2009), p 19, 20.
3. Gary J. Lovejoy, Ph.D and Gregory M. Knoph, M.D., *Light on the Fringe: Finding Hope in the Darkness of Depression*. (Published by In The Light Communications, 1977).
4. Zechariah 4:10 "For who has despised the day of small things?" (KJV).
5. Proverbs 17:22 "A cheerful heart makes good healing, but a stricken spirit dries the bone." (KJV).

# Sam & Debbie's To Do List ———✦

- ☑ Watch a Star Trek Episode (Debbie)
- ☑ Text a Friend (Debbie)
- ☑ Mow the Yard with Anthony (Sam)
- ☑ Meet With our Family Counselor (Sam and Debbie)
- ☑ Give Sam a Haircut (Anthony)

# Chapter Fourteen

## Recovery Room

### DEBBIE

*After* forty years of nursing I just can't help using the recovery room parallel. Losing a child is a unique experience for every parent. The age, emotional or spiritual condition of the person at the time of their death, your unique history with the person, how the death happened, what you observed, or the role you played in the events surrounding their death all create a unique blend of grieving ingredients and creates a unique path of recovery. Each of us needs a recovery room specially designed just for us.

Sam experienced losing a spouse (divorce is a form of death). He lost both a young, innocent child, and an adult, problematic step-son. He says each hurt, but in a different way, with a different intensity, and the path to recovery has been unique for each. Your history with and relationship to each person plays a role in forming its own distinctive grieving time, intensity and recovery.

# TIME HEALS ALL WOUNDS, OR DOES IT?

In the book of Ecclesiastes, chapter three, verse four, it says there is a time to mourn and a time to dance. Everyone's timetable is as unique as they are. Mourning and dancing are both powerful tools in helping us heal, but often the timing is as important as the ingredient. We have to take time to mourn. Considering how much time we mourn and how we mourn can be very healthy. Recognizing when we have crossed a healthy line is important in keeping us from inflicting more trauma upon ourselves.

We've all heard it said that time heals all wounds. Sam remembers once responding to someone who said that, "Time doesn't heal anything. Yes, certain things help us heal, time just gives us the space in which the healing balm can be applied. But we must intentionally search out the right balm, and choose to apply it, in the right amounts."

# SEEK INNER HEALING

Dr. Mark Virkler saw physical healings jump from ten percent to around a seventy percent success rate when he connected soul healing to healing of the body. What is going on in your heart greatly effects what is going on in your body, in your life and in your relationships. Mark and Patti Virkler's book, Prayers that Heal the Heart, and study course by the same name, can help bring a healing balm to your heart by understanding how the Holy Spirit heals wounds.[1] We don't hesitate to go to the doctor when we have pain. Do not hesitate to understand the healing Jesus wants to bring to your whole person. Jesus said:

*"He hath sent Me to heal the brokenhearted"*
LUKE 4:18 (KJV)

While the blend of balm ingredients is unique to each of us, there are certain ingredients that are universally healthy, which we can identify and choose to include in our unique journey. Some may need more forgiveness, while others require an infusion of hope. Some may need a change of scenery, while others need to clean the house. A great question is, where do we get help and perspective in deciding what ingredients we need in our unique blend?

Over my career in the hospital I've seen thousands of people recovering from a diversity of complications, with a wide range and length of recovery. And, as a nurse I was always observing the unique reaction of each patient to a medicine.

For some, the trauma seemed to take a larger toll and it took longer to recover. Others healed quickly and moved out of intensive care in a shorter time. Others reappeared later, still struggling to get above destructive patterns that had kept them emotionally weak and physically vulnerable.

In the larger view of working with hurting people for a lengthy career, I can see patterns emerge in those years of experience and I want to unwrap some healing "ointments" for you, if you will. I'd like to make some recovery process suggestions, my own unique R.N. (recovery navigations) extracted from my experience watching people of all shapes and sizes recover from all kinds of wounds.

## INTENTIONALLY CONSIDER YOUR REACTIONS

When you lose a child or a mate the pain lessens over time, but is always there. Love leaves us vulnerable and can open us to so many kinds of wounds. Some cope by simply shutting love out, others cope by seeking love too hard. It is always good to intentionally think about how we are doing, to take our emotional temperature, to take our spiritual blood pressure, to monitor our condition and how our coping mechanisms are doing.

For me it was actually more painful the second year after Zachary's funeral because I was numb the first year. The hardest time for a patient often happens when the anesthesia first wears off and they become fully aware of their pain and their condition. Fear often hits at this moment and takes its toll. Will I recover? How painful will this be? Will I ever get over it? Who will help me? Can I go it alone? How much help will I need? All these questions are good, but we need a structured, stable way to access our condition and progress, and decide our course of treatment. It's often there that we need the most help. So, here's my first R.N. suggestion: go ballroom dancing.

# RECOVERY ROOM 1
## GO BALLROOM DANCING

Sam and I went ballroom dancing again last month. It was a great return to an activity we loved and had been out of for a while. We were unable to do lessons or go dancing for about a year because of our commitment to Anthony, and all our grandkids.

It was great to see old friends and waltz through the evening with old love songs that helped pull positive emotions back to the center of my heart and push painful memories a little more out of my heart. Positive, fun activities that involve physical action, create new connections and recall good memories is a great way to recover. In this way pain will play a lesser role, and love a little larger role, in the life you will be building tomorrow.

What was even better, was to feel like waltzing through the night! But, oftentimes the feeling follows the action. You must not let the feelings make your decisions for you. There is a time to grieve, but there is also the time for joy, and it is not unusual or wrong to mix the two. So take action, against the negative feelings. Choose to go do something that will make you feel good about yourself and about your life. The feelings will follow the action.

## RECOVERY ROOM 2
### STAY CONNECTED

Remaining connected to just one close friend during tough times makes a huge difference. We are often so afraid to let our feelings show. We're afraid we'll lose control in public and others will see us as weak and will judge us or reject us. So, choose a close friend you can trust and let it all out! It's a great recovery technique. I know how valuable this is so I look for others who need to let it all out and I get them alone, ask a few questions, prod a little and then watch the damn burst. Helping them helps me. Whether helping or being helped, staying connected is the key.

## RECOVERY ROOM 3
### HELP OTHERS

On the road to recovery you can discover great answers that not only help you recover, but thereafter continue revolutionizing your life. Great relief can be found in developing a great passion for helping others. Who doesn't want to share what they love? When you discover hope, you want to share hope. Isaiah 40:31 says "... Those who hope in the Lord will renew their strength. They will soar on wings like eagles; they will run and not grow weary, they will walk and not faint." (NIV) I have a heart and passion for helping grandmothers, and moms and grandfathers too, because I love what helped me survive and thrive. So, I'm starting a blog called awesomegrandmothers.org.

So many are going through difficult times and need to know they're not alone and I know I can encourage them with the answers I have discovered. Grandmothers can save the next generation. How awesome is that?

# RECOVERY ROOM 4
## ACCEPTANCE

*"Our level of joy (and therefore strength and healing) is directly proportionate to our level of acceptance. Our attitude is the key,"*
—TIM HANSEL[2]

Remember Bella's dream I talked about earlier? I think it bears repeating for this important point. One day she said, "I had a dream about daddy." I thought how interesting. I asked, "Did your daddy say anything to you?" She shook her head yes and said, "He said, "Accept."" What an answer coming from a six-year old. I don't remember us ever talking with her about the idea of accepting what had happened, or using the word accept. Whether she really saw something or the Holy Spirit simply dropped the experience into her imagination we will never know, but this six-year-old might teach us adults something about inner healing.

In her book You Can Be Emotionally Free, Rita Bennet says, "This kind of prayer, in which we allow the Holy Spirit to inspire our creative imagination, can help in many ways. In it, He can create a brand-new memory, or He can create new scenes within an old memory."[3] Often we left brain adults think we must understand for something to work, when what we really need is to come to God in childlike faith and simply accept His work in us.

# RECOVERY ROOM 5
## DON'T FEAR FORGETTING

It's a natural thing to fear that you might forget someone you so loved. But, letting go and letting them move a little from the center is not forgetting. It's a natural part of the process of moving on with your life. Moving on with your life, doesn't mean you are losing their life. They lived their life, you cannot continue to live their life for them. Working too hard to keep them alive, is to short circuit your life.

You can keep their memory alive in healthy ways;

- Remember good times
- Laugh about the good times with a friend
- Do a scrap book
- Journal
- Exercise
- Join a Bible study
- Stay busy
- Keep some pictures out
- Clean out the closet
- Redecorate

Clean out the closet when you're ready. But, you must eventually clean out the closet. Yes, it can be painful, but cleaning can be a healthy part of healing. Just be aware of when any activity gets compulsive, controls you more than you control it. You can keep their memory alive. Don't worry. You will never forget. Relax!

*"Be still and know that I am God."*
PSALMS 46:10 (NIV)

# RECOVERY ROOM 6
## TOSS OUT GUILT AND SHAME – THE UGLY STEPSISTERS

Guilt and shame are twins that usually move in to our house in pairs. I did this wrong, I could have done that better, what if this would have happened differently? Obsessing on what could have been is like trying to make a fast getaway on a wooden horse. It may create a lot of motion, but you'll get nowhere, fast.

Guilt can become a lifestyle. Forgive yourself. Forgive God. Forgive other people. Whatever others have done wrong to you, lack of forgiveness is like inviting them into your home, making them your best friend, marrying them and becoming who they are. Forgiveness does not at all say that who they are or what they did is ok, but it does say, what you did will no longer harm me.

Shame for any fault in the transpiring of events is destructive, even if you are guilty. People find ways to punish themselves to the level of value they have given their loss. Some people never stop punishing themselves and they do it in all kinds of ways. Some make their "problem," their reaction to trauma so complex no answer can ever be found or work. In this case they have made the choice to continue to inflict self-wounding until they discover the pain is greater than the loss, that they are just tired of being tired.

# RECOVERY ROOM 7
## FIND BIBLICAL, HOLY SPIRIT LED COUNSELING

If the story of the garden of Eden teaches us anything, it teaches us that love without borders is destructive. You may have loved the person or the career you lost, you may still love them, but love unrestricted can become destructive. If you, or someone around you is caught up in a destructive pattern of any kind; excessive weight loss or spending, cutting, throwing things, yelling at people, wrecking cars, attempting suicide, seek out professional help! Call your pastor, let a friend in. There are ways to talk through it without costing a lot of money. Look for a church that offers counseling or research Christian, Bible based counselors in your area. Counselors have a wide range of knowledge and skill. If one counselor doesn't seem to be helping, seek out another until you find a good fit.

# RECOVERY ROOM 8
## JOURNALING

Writing helps bring perspective and balance to the events of the previous day. It helps you define what you saw and heard. It helps you express what you felt. It's a great way of letting out what has been forced into your mind. By its very definition a traumatic event will be strong and intrusive. It will make an impact on you either for the positive or for the negative. Journaling can decide what that role will be and to what intensity it will play in that role.

Journaling helps you decide what importance a yesterday event will play in your tomorrow life. When you write, your brain scrutinizes and organizes the previous day's events. In fact, during your eight hours of sleep your brain is going through all the previous day's events, organizing them, and cataloging them according to priority of importance and as a result of that process is deciding what is important enough to discard, or to keep and pack away in long term, unconscious memory.[4] Journaling helps you play a conscientious role in this process.

# RECOVERY ROOM 9
## DISTRACTIONS – RELIEF MECHANISMS

A healthy distraction is a good thing. One time Sam was struggling with his business and becoming obsessed with making things work, working too hard, too many hours and spending too much. While praying one day about his business the Holy Spirit said to him (Another way to say this is a brilliant flash of an idea strongly t-boned his usual thought pattern), "Learn how to invest in the stock market." God often uses this method, helping us defeat negatives by helping us refocus on positives so some time can pass while He fixes things. While Sam studied the stock market with a small group of men, God set about fixing things in his business without Sam nosing in too much. And, while studying how to invest the Holy Spirit showed Sam, from this unlikely source, changes he needed to make in how he was managing his company. Sometimes God sneaks answers up on us. Start a new hobby, or reach out to someone. Granpa Cratchet often says to a child, "This is my long time, close, bosom buddy, best friend, who I just met." You can never tell when you're about to meet your next best friend.

# RECOVERY ROOM 10
## READ A WIDE VARIETY OF SUBJECTS

You can read yourself to becoming a different person, into living a new life. Reading is a great mini-vacation getaway, but be careful and don't bury yourself in books. When anything becomes too dominating in your schedule you could be trying to bury your pain in extreme activity. I love Redeeming Love by Francine Rivers and the classics.

The Bible has been at the top of the best seller list long before there was a best seller list, ever since the beginning. There is a reason for that, it has everything; intrigue, love, romance, adventure, wisdom, defeat and victory, trauma and healing, and knowledge for living. It's precepts and stories are so universally true that if you line your general life up with its laws, your specific problems, whatever they are, will be lessoned and most likely fully solved given time.

Take a course on how to read and study the Bible. Fall in love with this book and you will learn how much God loves you, no matter what. The best thing you can do to understand the Bible is to get to personally know its author. Give your heart and mind to Jesus, learn about the work of the Holy Spirit, and your instruction book (Basic Instructions Before Leaving Earth) will open up to you.

# TAKE YOUR EMOTIONAL TEMPERATURE

Our list of helpful Recovery Rooms could go on forever. The point is to intentionally take your emotional temperature, your spiritual blood pressure and get someone to help you objectively look at how you're doing. If anything is out of balance seek help. We all seek the help of a good doctor for our bodies, why not seek help when we need help with our thoughts or our emotions. A great counselor is an awesome thing.

Take your life temperature by making your own Recovery Room list. Ask yourself, what are my feelings and how am I responding to those feelings? Ask, what is my coping mechanism? Is it working for me? Is it helping me or hurting me? Get an objective observer to help you evaluate.

## The Rest of the Story

I have hope for myself and others struggling through the heartaches and headaches of defeating death, drugs, and dealing with disasters, diapers and other daily dos. We all have to put one foot in front of the other, with rest and joy along the way.

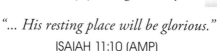

*"... His resting place will be glorious."*
ISAIAH 11:10 (AMP)

## SO NEXT SUMMER WHEN THE FLIP-FLOPS COME OUT, SO WILL MY PAINTED TOENAILS!

## ENDNOTES

1. Mark and Patti Virkler, *Prayers That Heal the Heart,* (Alachua, Florida, Published by Bride-Logos, 2009) The study course can be found at www.cluonline.org.
2. Tim Hansel, *You Gotta Keep Dancin',* (Elgin, Illinois: David C. Cook publishing company, 1985), p 105.
3. Rita Bennet, *You Can Be Emotionally Free,* (Alachua, Florida, Published by Bridge-Logos, 2007), p 86.
4. Dr. Caroline Leaf, *Who Switched Off My Brain: Controlling Toxic Thoughts and Emotions,* (Published by Improv Ltd, distributed by Thomas Nelson Publishers, USA, 2009).

# Debbie's Recovery Room To Do List

- ☑ Write a Blog
- ☑ Encourage Someone
- ☑ Think About How I Cope and Ask, "Is this Healthy?"
- ☑ Get my Toenails Painted
- ☑ Read a Great Book

# Let's Connect!

— ••• ❧ ☙ ••• —

Debra Susan Bowman is the creator of awesomegrandmothers.org, She blogs her experiences and shares her wisdom through real life stories that touch the heart and minister to the soul.

She also offers support to the many grandmothers who find themselves in the position of becoming mothers again as little ones are placed in their charge to raise. She is kind, caring, and filled with grace—connect with her today!

## READ DEBBIE'S BLOG!

AWESOME*Grandmothers*.org

Building Stable Families in a Challenging World

Samuel and Debbie Bowman are the founders of The Bowman Initiative and are dedicated to elevating the culture of business and family.

Sam conducts mentoring groups and provides training and resources for those in business, helping them assess where they are and apply the principles of wisdom in practical ways.

Debbie brings her experience and insight to the realm of the home, focusing on helping women of all ages strengthen the fabric of their families and provide encouragement and hope for those who have lost their way.

Together they have also created Granpa Cratchet and brought him to life, helping hundreds of thousands of children laugh and learn their way to a more positive future.

To learn more or to invite Sam or Debbie to speak at your event:

## BOWMANINITIATIVE.COM

# *Because*
# GRANPA SAYS SO
## *that's why!*

## Experience the Lighter Side of Business

- 600 of Granpa's Funniest One Liners!
- The Amusing Misadventures of Granpa's Performers
- Whimsical Trips Down Memory Lane
- Granpa's Photo Memories & Fun Facts
- The Hysterical History of How it All Happened
- … and so much more!

Available on amazon.com

Made in the USA
Middletown, DE
22 May 2017